A CENTURY OF HEROES

Edited By

Larry Wells

LONGSTREET PRESS
Atlanta, Georgia

This book is dedicated to the players, coaches, managers, trainers and fans of Ole Miss Football

Published by LONGSTREET PRESS, INC.
A subsidiary of Cox Newspapers,
A division of Cox Enterprises, Inc.
2140 Newmarket Parkway
Marietta, Georgia 30067

NOTE: Some of the articles in this book were previously published and are here reproduced by permission. By Willie Morris: "In the Spirit of the Game" (*Southern Living*, Nov. 1990); "Heroes in the Rain" (from *The Courting of Marcus Dupree*, University Press of Mississippi, 1992); Introduction (from *The Dog Comes Home*, Yoknapatawpha Press, 1984); *"Shootout at Legion Field,"* by Billy Watkins (The Clarion-Ledger).

Library of Congress Catalog Number 92-84005
ISBN: 1-56352-072-9

Printed in the United States of America
Book design by Gail Morton

CONTENTS

EDITOR'S NOTE

PERHAPS IT IS the abiding presence of Mississippi's Nobel Laureate and quarterback of the 1913 Oxford High B-Team, William Faulkner, that has drawn so many writers to Ole Miss and kept them here. When this book was conceived as a means of celebrating a hundred years of football at the University of Mississippi, we turned to writers associated with Ole Miss to share their memories with us. Literature and sports are not so far apart, after all, for heroes like Bruiser Kinard and Charlie Conerly and Archie Manning must have scribes to tell their stories. Barry Hannah is Ole Miss writer-in-residence and a longtime Rebel fan, despite his Choctaw and Razorback affiliations. John Grisham attended Ole Miss Law School after graduating from that "other" state university and lives in Oxford. Willie Morris, graduate of the University of Texas and Oxford University, spent ten years at Ole Miss as journalist-in-residence. Charles Overby attended Ole Miss and learned sports journalism from the "old master" himself, S.I.D. Billy Gates. David Sansing has taught history at the University since 1971 and is well-qualified to describe the Ole Miss mystique. Magazine executive and poet James Autry helped arrange funding of a magazine writing program but perhaps less well known are his exploits as drum major of the Rebel marching band. Dean Faulkner Wells, who was born in Oxford and attended Ole Miss, reveals how her father, Dean Faulkner (William Faulkner's youngest brother) was kicked off the 1925 team. William Winter, distinguished former governor of Mississippi, turns out to be a sportswriter in gubernatorial garb. Billy Watkins, feature writer for The Clarion-Ledger, writes eloquently of Ole Miss legend, Archie Manning. And since football and the arts have literally come together in the south end-zone of Vaught-Hemingway Stadium, I have undertaken to describe that phenomenon. Finally, this book was compiled under the overall direction of Assistant Athletic Director for Sports Information, Langston Rogers, a scribe for all seasons, who helped ride herd on an irrepressible, sometimes irreverent, bunch of Rebel writers.

L.W.

LITTLE did I know when I made the decision to accept a football scholarship to come to Ole Miss in 1956 that I would enjoy one of the most wonderful experiences a college football player could ever hope to enjoy. Having grown up in the small south Mississippi town of McComb, I had only been to Ole Miss on one or two occasions, but it didn't take me long to realize this was going to be a special place for me.

I could feel the spirit which existed among the students. With an enrollment of less than 4,000 at the time, we knew just about everybody. The students that we went to class with and went to dances with all supported the football team. They took the losses as hard as we did, but probably celebrated the victories a little more than we were allowed.

Warner Alford

Being a part of three teams with a combined record of 29-3-1, winning a conference championship, being on a team named national champion by the Football Writers Association, and being on the team picked SEC Team of the Decade in the 1950s, was really an unbelievable experience. Still, the honor which meant more to me than anything was being selected, along with Jake Gibbs, as one of the co-captains my senior year.

With two Miss Americas (Mary Ann Mobley and Lynda Lee Mead) back-to-back amid all of that football supremacy, it almost created a Camelot atmosphere in Oxford. You couldn't have drawn a blueprint for a college experience to be more satisfying and rewarding.

The coaching staff at that time was one of the best in the nation and Coach Vaught was ahead of his time as an offensive innovator, although I didn't realize it during my playing days. With only about 40 players on our travel squad, the feeling within our teams was one of great camaraderie.

Having been a part of 100 years of Ole Miss football is an awesome feeling. To have played here, been able to return as an assistant coach, and then remain as a part of the athletic department has provided me with so many wonderful moments. I'm so grateful I came to Ole Miss.

Warner Alford is Director of Athletics.

AS A youngster growing up in Columbus, Miss., I was exposed to Ole Miss football at an early age. We listened to the games on radio every week, but that was just not enough to satisfy a burning desire to actually see the Rebels.

Billy Brewer

One Saturday morning in 1952, I think I was in the seventh or eighth grade, my good friend Larry McKnight and I decided to hitchhike to Oxford for the Maryland game. We had heard all about how great Maryland was and some of our friends said Ole Miss didn't have a chance. Somewhere around Okolona, Dick Crago, the Ole Miss announcer, picked us up and took us to Oxford.

Since we didn't have a ticket and there wasn't a seat to be had, Larry and I went around to the back of the stadium and crawled under the fence. I don't know how it happened, but we finally ended up standing on the Maryland sideline and saw a great football game. Of course, Ole Miss won 21-14, which really put a not-so-well-known football program on the map. It was the most spirited and enthusiastic atmosphere I had ever experienced. I knew right then that I wanted to be a part of that excitement.

As a player and coach at Ole Miss, I have been fortunate to have been involved in so many great games. There were times when everything seemed lost, but we managed to find a way to win.

In recent years, as a coach, there was the Mississippi State game in 1983 when the wind miraculously knocked down the field goal and helped us earn a bowl invitation. The Alabama game in 1988 comes to mind as well as the 1989 Tulane game in New Orleans when we scored on the last play. And we will never forget the 1992 Mississippi State game where our defense reclaimed the Golden Egg by holding the Bulldogs out of the end zone for those 11 plays.

On the day we kicked off the year-long celebration of 100 years of Ole Miss football, my thoughts drifted back to that Saturday morning in 1952. It was the beginning of a journey which has provided me with so many great memories. My dream was to be an Ole Miss Rebel. I'm thankful that dream came true.

Billy Brewer is Head Football Coach.

OLE MISS FOOTBALL

100

A CENTURY OF HEROES

1893

1993

The Ole Miss Mystique

By David G. Sansing

The Ole Miss Mystique

A COUPLE of years ago I stopped at a service station in rural south Mississippi. It was a family-owned station which sold groceries on credit but did not honor credit cards of any kind. When the kindly old man who owned the station found out that I was from the University of Mississippi he became apologetic. He was sorry he could not accept my card and he told me, lowering his voice, if I was "running a little short," I could send it to him later. I thanked him for his kindness, paid him, and turned to leave when he said, "You're from Ole Miss, hunh." Since he already knew I was, he was not asking, and knowing it called for no response so I offered none. He continued in that quaint, sonorous, unreproduceable, rural Mississippi accent, "Yes, suh, I tell you this, I ain't a alma mater of Ole Miss, but it's sure my school." Repressing my professorial instinct to correct his misuse of the term alma mater, I confessed that I was not an alma mater either but told him with pride that my three children were. Then I asked him why he felt so strongly and so deeply about Ole Miss. He attempted, perhaps for the first time in his life, to translate his feelings into words, to verbalize his emotions. After a few minutes, seeing him grow uncomfortable in his verbal infelicity, I offered him the use of some colorful adjectives and a few compound nouns. Declining my offer he finally said, "Hell I don't know, I just love that place." Content to let it go at that, I got in the car to leave, but he was not through. He kept talking and gradually his tone changed and he was obviously more at ease as he began to make a speech about the Civil War, the Lost Cause, the federal government, about the Kennedy's, race, football, pretty girls, and Miss Americas. During a convenient pause, I told him that I really had to go. But before I left I told him of the distinguished list of Rhodes Scholars Ole Miss had produced. I thought he might use that information in some future oration.

The next day I had an interview with a Jackson business executive who was an Ole Miss alumni. Amid the luxury of corporate headquarters, I asked this distinguished alumni the same question I had asked the good old boy. The articulate

David G. Sansing

Ole Miss alumni do not just stroll through The Grove, they retrace the steps of their forebears, not just over place and space but back through time as well. Frank Everett is quite right when he says that students may graduate from the University of Mississippi but they never leave Ole Miss . . . It is their link, their nexus to who they were and are.

and erudite executive made a speech remarkably similar to the one I had heard the day before, with one exception. He knew about the Rhodes Scholars. After saying all the obvious things an alumnus says about his alma mater, his erudition gave way to emotion and his practiced diction gave way to dialect, "Hell, it ain't easy to explain how I feel about Ole Miss and how much it means to me."

I once heard a man say, "I love my family and all that, but I really love Ole Miss."

The fondness Ole Miss alumni have for this place amazes me. It is more than the filial affection alumni have for their alma mater. It goes beyond that, much deeper. It is almost like a spell, or magic, it's metaphysical and mystical. All alumni do not have this same feeling, and it seems much stronger among older alumni than in more recent graduates. But those who are possessed of this feeling seem somehow bound by it; it becomes a commitment, a promise, an oath to be honored with a faithful fidelity. Perhaps the best way, maybe the only way, to explain this phenomenon is to say that the Ole Miss Mystique has them under its spell.

I don't think I can define the Ole Miss Mystique but I have seen it work its way, wrap itself around, charm, disarm, and intrigue people who encounter it for the first time.

The Ole Miss Mystique both borrows from and lends to the Mississippi Mystique. People in other parts of the country who meet

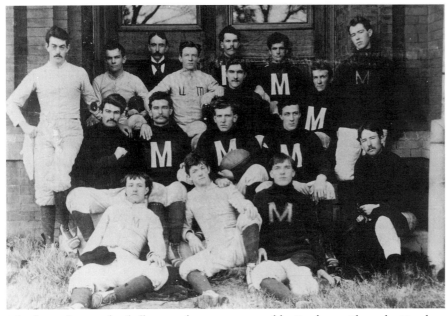

The first Ole Miss football team of 1893, organized by Professor Alexander Bondurant.

JOHN BIGGS

Coach Billy Brewer after the 1989 Liberty Bowl.

one of us for the first time seem intrigued to find a real, live Mississippian outside his natural habitat. I experienced this in the crowded customs office of New York's Kennedy Airport where I had gone to meet a group of German students. Acting as urbane as I could and concealing as much of my Mississippi accent as possible, I addressed the customs official who most nearly gave the impression that he knew what was going on. When I told him that I was from the University of Mississippi he asked, "Is that the same as Ole Miss?" Responding in my native dialect, I said, "Yes, Suh!" He then told me he knew all about Ole Miss because a young lady in his office had gone to school there for two years. He confessed he had never known any-one to love a place as much as she had loved Ole Miss. Because of her, and her fondness for Ole Miss, he would see that we got through cus-toms with minimal delay.

I think I saw the Ole Miss

Bookends of a dynasty and the architect behind it: Archie Manning, John Vaught and Charlie Conerly.

Two All-America linemen whose careers span the history of Ole Miss football: Bruiser Kinard and Ben Williams.

Three Miss Americas for Ole Miss: Mary Ann Mobley (1959), Susan Akin (1986) and Lynda Lee Mead (1960).

Mystique in the fascination of a young black scholar from the Midwest who attended a symposium on slavery at the University. As I drove him around the campus and through Oxford, he was intrigued by this place and its past. His interest was probably as much emotional as academic. I think I saw the Ole Miss Mystique at work among a group of Japanese journalists who came to see where William Faulkner lived and to look at the people he wrote about. "Did you know him," they asked? Unfortunately, I did not.

A mystique does not combust. It evolves long before it envelops. The Ole Miss Mystique was long aborning and the stuff it's made of is the stuff of place and past.

Almost five years before the University was established a town was founded by some people who believed that there is something in a name. Seeking every possible advantage, they named their town Oxford in the hope that it would be selected as the site for the new state University. By a vote of 58 to 57 the legislature located the University at Oxford in Lafayette County rather than at Mississippi City in Harrison County. It is not likely the Ole Miss Mystique would have evolved along the sandy shores of the gulf as it did here amid the hallowed groves.

At about the time the University was established and the sons of Mississippi's gentry were shaping the traditions of Ole Miss, Matthew Arnold wrote these lines about Oxford University:

> So steeped in sentiment as she
>   lies,
> Spreading her gardens to the
>   moonlight,
> And whispering the last enchant-
>   ments of the Middle Ages

Ole Miss also whispers the last enchantments of an earlier age. Not to understand that is not to under-stand the mystique which surrounds it or the history which has shaped it.

On the occasion of its twenty-fifth anniversary, Chancellor John Waddell addressed the graduating class: "This university has my heart's affections. She was my first love. When the touch of death shall lay me in the grave, then let me sweetly sleep beneath the shadow of her fame and these classic groves."

Twenty-five years later, after the University of Mississippi had become known as Ole Miss, a student poet refrained:

> A thousand leagues of prairie
> Between my heart and bliss;
> How can it then be merry,
> Beloved Ole Miss?

ROBERT JORDAN

ROBERT JORDAN

Dr. Gerre Hopkins and Archie Manning at the 1970 LSU game

How strong so'er I be
I needs must weep at this;
Thy hallowed groves I see
No more, Ole Miss!

Let fortune smile on me,
Or O'er my failures hiss
As I am true to thee
Or false, Ole Miss.

The mystique was evolving. But first came war with its pestilence, then progress with all its perils. But rather than endangering the place where Ole Miss was, both war and progress endeared it. Monuments were raised to the heroes of the Lost Cause. There is a Confederate cemetery on the campus, and a memorial to the University Greys. This place became hallowed ground. During the lumber boom following the Civil War the virgin pines were plucked from those classic groves, but the oaks remained. They too are monuments, safe even from progress.

In 1928 Governor Theodore Bilbo wanted to move the University of Mississippi to Jackson. On the basis of practical economics, the proposal was sound. However, Mississippians, as one writer put it, were "infidels in the fold of good business." They practiced an "agnostic faith in a sort of irresponsibility" which exempted their leaders from the rigors of responsible statecraft. Decisions of consequence were not to be made on the basis of practical economics. Mississippians expected

10

1941 freshmen backs: Charlie Conerly, Doug Kenna, Ray Woodward, Leonard Stagg.

Coach Steve Sloan and quarterback John Fourcade.

their leaders to be moved by higher and nobler impulses. Chancellor Alfred Hume certainly appealed to those nobler impulses in his 1928 speech urging the legislature not to move the University:

The University of Mississippi is rich in memories...If its children do not come to its defense the very stones in the memorial arches and Confederate monument would cry out...The memorial window in the old library erected in loving memory of the University Greys, the Confederate monument near by, and the Confederate Soldier's Cemetery a little further removed, are as sacred as any ancient shrine, alter, or temple. Instead of moving the University away, that it might be a little easier to reach, ought not the people of Mississippi to look upon a visit

11

here as a holy pilgrimage?...Gentlemen, you may move the University of Mississippi. You may move it to Jackson or any where else. You may uproot it from [this] hallowed ground ... but gentlemen, don't call it Ole Miss.

Sentiment and sense of place prevailed over practical economics and the relocation plan was abandoned. Although the decision was ridiculed by some, Mississippi's disdain for progress and practical economics was seen by one writer as "a kind of stark and lonely grandeur in [a] docile world."

And so the University remained here amidst those classic groves and became an "outpost of the quiet splendors of the old regime." And the Ole Miss Mystique evolved.

If Mississippians have a sense of place they surely have a sense of history; a foreboding sense of destiny from which they derive a need for continuity. In a world of ravishing changes, Ole Miss alumni do not just stroll through the grove, they retrace the steps of their forebears, not just over place and space but back through time as well. Frank Everett is quite right when he says that students may graduate from the University of Mississippi but they may never leave Ole Miss. For Ole Miss is more than their alma mater. It is their link, their nexus to who they were and are, and where they came from. They are in subconscious contact with their past.

"Who in the hell are we — Ole Miss by damn!" This is not a question, it is a confirmation.

With that confirmation comes the gift of poetry and prophesy. As poets the confirmed have license with rhyme and meter, and weights, measures, and numbers. They train their gift of prophesy not on the future but on the past. To adherents, to the true believers, the saddest words of tongue or pen are: "what might have been." It is "what might have been" that captivates the Ole Miss alumni.

To understand the Ole Miss Mystique one must understand "what might have been." And "what might have been" happened a long time ago, amid "the quiet splendors of the old regime."

When the peace of those halcyon days of long ago was disturbed by the clanking of countervailing ideas, the statesmen of the old regime built their own University where their sons could study the art of statecraft free from corrupting influences. The old regime was under siege.

When the ideological siege gave way to mortal combat, their University became an early casualty. Every student at the University of Mississippi enlisted in the army of the old regime. On the afternoon of July 3, 1863, Company A, 11th Mississippi, known as the University Greys, won "imperishable glory" at Gettysburg in defense of "principles inherited from their fathers and strengthened by the teaching of their alma mater." At Gettysburg, "what might have been" happened. The University Greys scaled that fateful rim of Cemetery Ridge, forty-seven yards in advance of Pickett's charge. Their advance is considered the "high

(1976) Ole Miss 10 - Alabama 7.

water mark of the Confederacy." Of the few survivors, none returned to the University and no reunion was ever held. There is only a memorial to them in Ventress Hall—a stained glass window, a beautiful but fragile reminder. There are other Confederate Memorials on campus. One is a cemetery where 600 young men, Confederate and Union, rest in a common grave where "what might have been" no longer matters.

"What might have been" belongs to the living; it is their responsibility. The speaker at the 1867 commencement urged the University's graduating class to preserve "in fragrant memory that peculiar civilization which has been an ornament of the South, but which is now to pass away." He also urged them to transmit to posterity in permanent form a "record of the struggle just closed."

Or else, he warned, "we have no security for the future against a thraldom far worse than that of the bayonet."

From the ruins of the old regime a New South and a New Mississippi emerged. The small farmers and laborers in the northeast hills and the Piney Woods finally wrested political control from the Delta and river counties. The gentry's hegemony was broken. During that bitter political struggle, the issue of class often surfaced. It was inevitable that the University would be brought into that struggle. The small farmers and common laborers, who were called Rednecks, accused the state university of pampering the sons of the gentry and neglecting the education of the sons and daughters of the working class. Eventually, Mississippi A & M College and Mississippi State College for Women were established to provide vocational training for the young white men and women of Mississippi. Recognizing in a limited way its responsibility for providing higher education for its black youth, the state also established Alcorn University.

At Mississippi A & M and MSCW all students wore uniforms and Greek societies with exclusive memberships were prohibited. The practice of exclusion was a relic of aristocracy and was not in keeping with the purpose for which those institutions were founded. At the University, however, Greek societies flourished. And the Ole Miss Mystique evolved.

In 1897 the Greek societies held a contest to select a name for their annual publication. The winning entry was Ole Miss and the yearbook became a powerful agent in the evolution of the Ole Miss Mystique. The 1918 edition of the Ole Miss was dedicated to the young men in military service. The editor extolled the courage of those valiant soldiers who showed fidelity "to the teaching of [their] chivalric forbears" in "the cause of honor, home, and humanity." He compared their heroic deeds to those of the University Greys and pledged that they, like the Greys, would never be forgotten.

The student newspaper was also a force in the evolution of the mystique. When some university students were criticized for using "unparliamentary adjectives" at a sporting event, the editor scolded them: "We as students of the University represent the cream of Mississippi youth, the flower of Mississippi families. We are supposed to have been reared in homes where elegance of manners and language is atmospherical...We must leave [profanity] for those yokels whose asininity is congenital...We must remember that the finest families of the commonwealth are represented among Ole Miss students." This editorial was written in 1930 and it was not a parody.

By the 1930s the Ole Miss Mystique was evolving apace. Since the inauguration of football as an intercollegiate sport in 1893, the Ole Miss team had been called the Red and Blue. These colors were selected by Professor Alexander Bondurant, a Latin scholar and the team's first coach. This lackluster, if colorful, designation did not capture the fancy of those who were coming increasingly under the spell of the Ole Miss Mystique. The student paper conducted a contest in 1929 to select a name for the University's athletic teams which would "symbolize the spirit, traditions, and ideals of the University of Mississippi." The 800 entries included Young Massers, Magnolians, Confederates, Invincibles, and Mississippi Mudders. The winning entry was "Mississippi Flood." Democrats and Rebels tied for second and Ole Marsters came in third. However, the name Flood failed to catch on.

It was hardly used at all in the 1930s.

On May 2, 1936, the student newspaper announced another contest. From the 600 entries a committee selected forty names. The forty names were eventually reduced to five. The five final names were sent to forty-two sports writers who were asked to rank them according to their preference. Within a few months Ole Miss had a name that captured the fancy of those who like to think about "what might have been." The name Rebel was selected. In 1937 a variation of Colonel Rebel appeared on the cover of the Ole Miss and Rebel flags which first appeared during the 1940s were omnipresent by the fifties.

All the stuff that mystiques are made of was present in the late 1940s: a place, with its hallowed ground; a past, with its reflections of imperishable glory; and symbols, which issued not from imagination but from memory Some great triumph, a string of victories won under those symbols and the mystique would envelop.

Then came the glory days when the Ole Miss Rebels won several conference championships, started a string of bowl games, were named the Southeastern Conference team of the decade for the 1950s, and won "imperishable glory" with a national championship in 1960. The Ole Miss Mystique enveloped.

In those glory days it was on the gridiron not the diamond or the court where the Ole Miss Rebels won their "imperishable glory." Football is a grand and colorful spectacle. The great crowds, the banners, the symbols, the bands, and the music spark our martial instincts. Every time I go to an Ole Miss football game and see the Rebels take the field and hear Dixie and see all the flags I am reminded of something Faulkner wrote:

It's all now you see. Yesterday won't be over until tomorrow and tomorrow began ten thousand years ago. For every Southern boy fourteen years old, not once but whenever he wants it, there is the instant when it's still not yet two o'clock on that July afternoon in 1863, the brigades are in position behind the rail fence, the guns are laid and ready in the woods and the furled flags, are already loosened to break out and Pickett himself with his long oiled ringlets and his hat in one hand probably and his sword in the other looking up the hill waiting for Longstreet to give the word and it's all in the balance, it hasn't happened yet, it hasn't even begun yet, it not only hasn't begun yet there is still time for it not to begin against the position and those circumstances which made more men than Garnett and Kemper and Armstead and Wilcox look grave yet it's going to begin, we all know that, we have come too far with too much at stake and that moment doesn't even need a fourteen-year-old boy to think this time. Maybe this time with all this much to lose and all this much to gain: Pennsylvania, Maryland, the world, the golden dome of Washington itself to crown with desperate and unbelievable victory the desperate gamble.

During the Glory Days the image of Ole Miss became superim-

posed upon the public's perception of the University. It was here at Ole Miss that Mississippi experienced its greatest triumphs, its brightest moments, and to some, its darkest hours. The Ghosts of Ole Miss still haunt this University—- Johnny Vaught, Archie Manning, Mary Ann Mobley, Lynda Lee Mead, all those Rhodes Scholars, and James Howard Meredith.

In 1962 the whispers gave way to epithets, and the lonely outpost became a battleground. Change like a terrible swift sword came to Mississippi and even Ole Miss was not free from it or could withstand it. But Ole Miss endured that change and in the intervening years the University has prevailed, not in spite of but because of that change.

The admission of African-Americans to this institution has enlarged it, enhanced it, enriched it, and enlightened it. Who would have imagined on that dark night in 1962 that the grandson of Mohandas Ghandi would come to the University of Mississippi in 1987 to study race relations in America. Who would have believed that Ole Miss's most recent Rhodes scholar would be Damon Moore. Who would have believed that "Gentle Ben" Williams would be an All-American and Colonel Rebel, or that Chucky Mullins would become a Favorite Son of Mississippi. Who could have imagined in the aftermath of the Meredith riot that in its centennial season Ole Miss would start a black quarterback, or that when the team takes its ceremonial walk through

16

The Grove half of the players are African Americans. A new Ole Miss Mystique is evolving.

Both borrowing from and lending to the evolution of the new Ole Miss Mystique are Head Football Coach Billy Brewer and his wife Kay. In their own special way Kay and Billy have widened the circle of the Ole Miss family and Coach Brewer has restored the Ole Miss football program to national prominence.

In 1983 when Billy Brewer returned to his alma mater as head coach, the faithful may have hoped but few believed that Ole Miss would be playing in a New Year's Day bowl game or go to five bowls and be ranked in the top twenty within the next decade, or that Billy would three times be named SEC Coach of the Year, or that he would survive long enough in the toughest conference in the country to become Dean of the SEC coaches. The final chapter on Billy Brewer will be written in the Book of Legend and he, too, will someday be a Ghost of Ole Miss.

The Ole Miss Mystique evolves anew.

To Be a Scrub

By Dean Faulkner Wells

To Be a Scrub

AS MY friend Willie Morris likes to observe, "The Faulkners are a bit on the small side." My family's stature, or the lack of it, did not significantly affect anyone as far as I know, until my father's size got him kicked off the Ole Miss football team.

Dean Faulkner Wells

Dean Swift Faulkner was five foot eight and weighed perhaps one hundred and twenty-five pounds when he entered Ole Miss in 1925. Having played quarterback for the Oxford High School team he had dreams of playing for the University, then known as the Ole Miss "Red and Blue." I don't know if my grandfather Murry Falkner pushed him to play, but no doubt Murry's lifelong interest in sports had something to do with Dean's desire to play college football. But I suspect it was the taste of gridiron glory from his high school days that made Dean so determined to make the Ole Miss team.

At first, Dean took football pretty casually, as he did nearly everything except golf and bird hunting. When he was in high school, cool autumn days presented a pleasant crisis: whether to spend his afternoons on the football field or in the woods, hunting. Most days he chose football.

In the 1920s Oxford High School football was extremely informal. The games were sometimes played on a flat, dusty field behind the high school [located at the site of the present Federal Building]. The field was hardpacked (if the weather was good—if not, it was a "sea of mud"). The field was bordered by "the Ditch," a fifteen-to-twenty foot gulley which dropped off into a sewer. The Ditch presented many problems. For example, the rules of the game at the time dictated that the ball must be played where it lay. However, at Oxford High School, if the ball wound up on the wrong side of the ditch, they were in a mess. Many a play was specifically designed in the huddle

Dean was too stubborn to give up and yet at every practice he was getting run over by the larger boys . . . Sullivan succinctly concluded, "He's going to get himself knocked in the head and killed."

Dean Faulkner Wells is the daughter of Dean Swift Faulkner, William Faulkner's youngest brother, who was killed in a plane crash at age 28 a few months before his daughter was born. Much of this article is based on interviews in Wells's masters thesis at the University of Mississippi.

Ventress Hall (housed law school, later the geology department); note Barnard Observatory in the background.

simply to get the ball back in the middle of the field. The games were usually attended by no more than thirty or so spectators, who made up for their lack of numbers with their enthusiasm. Since there were no bleachers, the fans followed every play by moving up and down the sidelines, staying even with the line of scrimmage, shouting encouragement (and offering suggestions to the coaches).

Most parents chose not to attend. One notable exception was Henry Minor Faser's father. His roar "That's my boy!" could be heard on the Square. Often Dr. Faser would race down the sidelines alongside the field, shouting "Run, Henry, run!" and score his own touchdown before Oxford High had snapped the ball.

Dean was Oxford's 120-pound quarterback. Fortunately, some of the linemen who blocked for him were bigger, "all the way up to 190 pounds," one of his teammates once told me, "and one boy in particular saved Dean's neck on more than one Friday afternoon. His name was Henry Lawhorne. He killed himself running interference for Dean, time and time again. He just didn't want to see Dean get hurt, so he looked after him like a chicken." Occasionally Oxford High had access to the Ole Miss field, and local news clippings attest to spirited prep games on the campus:

October 3: Oxford High School and the Lafayette County Aggies battled evenly...with the O.H.S.

boys getting a victory 7 to 6. Falkner's long end run was a high light on the Oxford offense.

October 9: Oxford High defeated Grenada High School...in an exciting game by the score of 13 to 7....The stars of the contest for Oxford were Faser, Falkner, Lawhorn....

November 21: In the first high school game of the season on the Ole Miss campus, Oxford High School defeated Holly Springs High School by a score of 33 to 0. Although outweighed, Oxford completely outplayed the Holly Springs aggregation. Falkner, quarterback for the Oxford team, was the star, making many long, spectacular gains, one of a 40 yard run for a touchdown. A large crowd of university students and town people witnessed the game.

All of the players, however, were not as devoted to Dean as Lawhorne had proved to be, especially one of them, who was closer to Dean in size. The competition for starting

Coach Homer Hazel brought "Big East" football to Ole Miss from Rutgers.

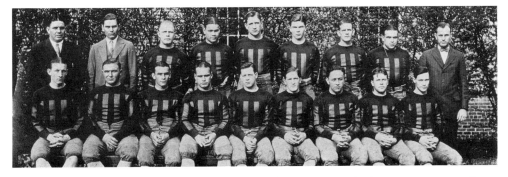

The 1925 Ole Miss varsity football team, in Coach Homer Hazel's first year, went 5-5, losing to Mississippi A & M by 0-6.

Halfback Tad Smith (for whom the Ole Miss coliseum is named) completes a pass to Lacy Byles. Smith was a close friend of Dean Swift Faulkner.

The 1926 season began with a bang as quarterback Hubby Walker (above) led Ole Miss to a 28-0 victory over the Arkansas State Aggies.

positions (and among fathers on the sidelines) was fierce, and two players who often were pitted against each other in practice were Henry Minor Faser, Jr., and Dean. Faser later recalled the competition:

"Since there were only fourteen boys on the squad, every player played both ways. Dean and I were both in the backfield when we had the ball, and when the opposing team was punting we played safety. One afternoon, during practice, the coach had us running back punts. Dean and I alternated, and when not running punts back, one of us would go down under the punts on defense. On one of Dean's times for running them back, I tackled him and got his shoe in my mouth, which broke off the corner of one tooth, and that tooth is still missing the edge."

Dean's fiercely competitive spirit led him to go out for football as an Ole Miss freshmen in 1925. It must have seemed a natural transition since he had played on the Ole Miss field in high school. Also, his father Murry Falkner was the University's business manager, and the family lived in the old Delta Psi fraternity house on campus [located near where the Alumni House now stands]. Dean's introduction to higher education caused very little change in his daily routine. He had walked back and forth to the high school (even going home for lunch) and now he continued to do the same. His attitude toward academics was the same as it had been throughout his high school career. His classes (the ones he chose to attend) met not far from the Delta Psi House where he continued to live, and his classmates included many longtime friends from Oxford. In those days Ole Miss students went to class from eight until noon on weekdays. Dean's first semester coursework included chemistry, English, mathematics, drawing, and surveying. In addition to these classes, all students were required to take Bible class, the one course in which it was said that "anyone worth his salt" was required, by peer pressure, to cheat.

Ole Miss was very small during the Roaring Twenties, with a total enrollment of about 800, including the medical school then located on

A student riot occurred when Ole Miss beat Mississippi State (A & M) 7-6 in 1926, and the Golden Egg trophy came into being as a means of keeping the peace.

Dean Swift Faulkner lettered in baseball, not football, at Ole Miss.

the Oxford campus. In a university
of that size, everybody knew everybody. Amusements were scarce, and
students had to be inventive when it
came to social life. During rush
week, for instance, a commonly
scheduled event was 'coon hunts in
Bailey's Woods near the campus.
Fraternity men would bring their
hunting dogs to school every fall
and take the rushees into the woods,
sit around a fire, bring out a bottle
and listen to the dogs running.
When a 'coon or a 'possum was
treed, the boys might or might not
stir themselves to go see it. Another
primary amusement was the arrival
and departure of daily passenger
trains. When students had nothing
else to do, they could always "wait
on the train just to see who got off."
Few students owned cars back then,
and a date often consisted of walking from the campus into town to
see a movie at the Ritz or Lyric
Theatre. America's best-known athletes were Babe Ruth, Red Grange,
Bill Tilden and Bobby Jones. Dean
and his friends listened to the radio
broadcast of the Dempsey-Firpo

heavyweight fight, along with a crowd of a hundred other boxing fans standing outside the Ritz Theatre on Depot Street [Van Buren Avenue, then not paved].

In pre-television days, as now, sports were an all-important diversion and football was the main attraction in the fall. The SEC had not yet been formed and Ole Miss was a member of the Southern Conference. Fellow members included Tulane, Vanderbilt, Alabama, Sewanee, Mississippi A & M (State), Auburn, Tennessee, Vanderbilt, Kentucky, Georgia, Georgia Tech, Florida and L.S.U.

The Ole Miss head coach was Homer Hazel, who had played his college football at Rutgers. As soon as classes were underway, Dean was extremely eager to try out for the team. He showed up at the first practice session, all 5'8" and 125 pounds. The freshmen "scrubs" primarily served as a scout team which the varsity scrimmaged against. For some reason, Freshman Coach R.L. Sullivan inserted Dean into the line-up at guard. He lasted three weeks.

Coach Sullivan and Murry Falkner had been good friends for years. Sullivan, who had played for Central Missouri, had been the head coach at Ole Miss before Homer Hazel. One October evening Sullivan showed up at the old Delta Psi House and asked to speak to Murry. The two men greeted each other cordially and stepped out on the porch. They chatted about the team's prospects for the season, then Sullivan came to the point.

Dean was the "best quarterback prospect" he had, but the problem was that "Dean's too little. That's just all there is to it." He told Murry that Dean was going to have to leave the team and asked Murry's help in persuading his son. Dean was too stubborn to give up and yet at every practice he was getting run over by the larger boys. He just didn't know when to quit. Sullivan succinctly concluded, "He's going to get himself knocked in the head and killed."

Calling Dean the "best quarterback prospect" was probably flattery on Sullivan's part to assuage Murry's disappointment, but it worked. Murry sat down with Dean the next day and convinced him to "save his natural talents and energies for baseball." Dean reluctantly agreed to delay his sports debut at the University until spring. His Ole Miss football career had ended.

Under Coach Hazel, the 1925 Red and Blue won five and lost five, beating Mississippi College and Millsaps but losing to Mississippi A & M in Jackson, 6 to 0. Dean went on to letter in baseball and did not seem to mind that his football "career" at Ole Miss had been so brief. However, I must have inherited some errant football gene from him. Not long ago I was playing tennis with Coach Jim Carmody's wife, Noonie. She remarked that Jim was recruiting defensive linemen all over the state. When I jokingly volunteered to play noseguard for Ole Miss, Noonie said, "You're mean enough, Dean. You're just not big enough."

Rebel with a Cause

R. HAPES
Halfback

KINARD
Tackle

POOLE
End

By Charles Overby

Rebel with a Cause

Charles Overby

HE NEVER TOSSED a pass, never ran a play, never made a tackle, never walked the sidelines as a coach. He wore glasses so thick that the football players used to joke that the astronomy department borrowed his lenses on cloudy nights.

But he did more to shape the national image of Ole Miss football for five decades than any other person.

Billy Gates, creator and keeper of football legends and lore, put Ole Miss on the map for sportswriters around the country as the athletic department's sports information director. From behind the scenes, Gates dominated the way people talked about Ole Miss football teams from the 1930s through the 1970s.

Consider just a few milestones:

—The nickname "Rebels" came from a Gates-sponsored contest when he was sports editor of The Mississippian in 1936.

—Twenty-one All-Americas, playing without the benefit of a major media market, gained national recognition from Gates' promotional efforts.

—Game statistics and records of individual achievements, now considered a basic part of playing football, were given painstaking emphasis and unprecedented clarity by Gates.

—Annual Rebel Guides set the standard nationwide for previewing and promoting football teams with a specialized publication.

In an age now dominated by big-budget promotional campaigns and high-tech wizardry, the one-man show of Billy Gates would be hard to recognize, even harder to duplicate.

Oh, he had a little help—a rag-tag student or two each year looking for a chance to pursue their dreams by working their way through school. Students like me.

Billy Gates, the gruffest public relations man I ever met, adopted kids like me and gave us a chance to do more than earn a few dollars. He let us touch and feel for the first time national greatness: the legendary, big-time Ole Miss football machine, an invention that meant more to many

"The University of Mississippi football team needs a new name. Once called the Flood and more lately the Red and Blue, it is now a man without a country, a child without a home. It has no real nickname with which to be properly identified."

—Billy Gates

31

Billy Gates

the Deep South, so much so that the specter of raging water left its mark on at least a few football teams: the Tulane Green Wave, the Alabama Crimson Tide and the Mississippi Flood.

Coach Ed Walker didn't think much of the Flood. Sportswriters were equally blasé about Red and Blue. Mississippi, the word, challenged headline writers enough, without the wordy Red and Blue.

In 1936, a young Jacksonian edited the sports pages of The Mississippian. He entered Ole Miss as a sophomore.

"Daddy loved Ole Miss so much that the first time he saw the campus, he went home and told his parents he wanted to transfer from Millsaps," recalls his son, Bill Gates, now an insurance executive in Memphis.

Gates lived at the only place available on campus—the band dormitory. He didn't read a note of music, but he talked his way in as a cymbals player.

Even as a student, Gates said—and wrote—what he thought. He thought the school nickname was lousy.

I have my own image—just a guess—of Gates sitting at his typewriter in early May of 1936 preparing to write a story for The Mississippian. As former sports editor of The Mississippian, I know that May is a dog month for writing sports. No football or basketball—even spring football has passed.

So Gates was probably drumming his fingers across the desk, trying to come up with an idea for his column.

Mississippians than the cotton gin.

By seeing up close the inner workings of this often mystical machine, we began to understand the literary imagery of the Wizard of Oz. Once you entered the basement office of the sports information department and parted the curtain, there was no all-powerful Wizard barking out orders. There wasn't much there at all. Just Billy Gates and a typewriter.

For five decades, it was more than enough.

THE HISTORIC floods of the 1920s had taken their toll in

Two-time (1936-37) All-America tackle Bruiser Kinard

Tom Swayze, end

James "Buster"
Poole, end

When he thought of the wimpy nick-names attached to the Ole Miss foot-ball team, he knew he could wring a column out of that without too much work. Probably knocked it off in less than an hour and headed to the golf course.

Gates loved golf and would later coach the Ole Miss golf team briefly—but long enough to lay claim to being the golf coach when Cary Middlecoff of Memphis played on the team. Middlecoff achieved greatness on the PGA tour. Gates' greatest claim to golf fame was shooting a 34 on the old Ole Miss nine-hole golf course the day his daughter, Tina, was born.

With the golf course beckoning, Gates probably was looking out on one of these classic cloudless May days in Oxford. In a moment of inspiration and need, he reached for a ploy that could give him not one, but two or more columns for the future, possibly enough to carry him to the end of the school year. A contest, yes, a contest would get him to the first tee long before dark and give him a chance to take a shot at that dumb nickname at the same time.

He kicked off the contest by writing: "The University of Mississippi football team needs a new name. Once called the Flood and more lately the Red and Blue, it is now a man without a country, a child without a home. It has no real nick-name with which to be properly iden-tified."

If Gates expected to be flooded with entries and reader comments that would provide the basis for

1936 Orange Bowl starting lineup—"The 1935 Ole Miss Red and Blue": (l-r) Claude Jackson, re; Bruiser Kinard, rt; Alex Breyer, rg; Charles Nelson, c; Dave Wilson, lg; Bill Richardson, lt; Jim "Buster" Poole, le; (standing) Coach Ed Walker; Ned Peters, hb; Dave Bernard, fb, Rab Rodgers, hb; Ray Hapes, hb.

future columns, he was quickly disappointed. Students were enjoying the prelude to summer too much to write or to care.

A true PR huckster of the 1930s—maybe the 1990s—would have made up a bunch of nicknames and started a ground swell for his personal favorite. But similar to his honest efforts of the future, Gates had no private agenda, nor did he seek to promote himself through the contest.

In fact, in the next week's issue, Gates declared the effort a failure: "The name contest started last week by The Mississippian seems to have failed utterly in stirring a response from the student body." He would have ditched the idea, but Coach Walker urged him to try again.

This time, he turned to sports editors around the state and the South, and their columns brought about 600 suggestions from the public, including one from Ben Guider of Vicksburg: Mississippi Rebels. A committee narrowed the list to five: Ole Miss Rebels, Ole Miss Raiders, Ole Miss Confederates, Ole Miss Stonewalls, and simply Ole Miss.

Indicative of the thinking of the time, all five nicknames leaned heavily on Mississippi's Old South/Civil War heritage. Guider, an attorney, said the Civil War connection would make the Rebel name popular:

". . . the name recalls to mind the glories of the Old South and that historic struggle of the Civil War in which the State of Mississippi took so

Ole Miss team boards bus for Tuscaloosa.

noble and outstanding a part, and for which every Mississippian should feel proud. Inasmuch as so many sections of our state are rich in tradition and memory of classic battles of that famous war, this name seems to me to be closely and peculiarly identified with the state of Mississippi, just as much so as the 'Cavaliers' of Virginia, 'Gators' of Florida and 'Gamecocks' of South Carolina."

Eighteen of 21 Southern sports writers voted for "Ole Miss Rebels." When the full Athletic Committee voted, Ole Miss Rebels narrowly edged Ole Miss, 4-3.

Chancellor A.B. Butts wrote to Gates on June 30, 1936 to confirm the selection. "As there are seven members on this committee," Butts wrote, "you will see that the majority vote for Ole Miss Rebels—a very small majority, however."

It's hard to imagine a student editor's idea carrying that kind of clout today. The Gates contest secured his place in the history of Ole Miss football. But he was just beginning.

THE EVOLUTION to big-time football began in 1936 when Ole Miss was invited to the Orange bowl and was narrowly defeated by Catholic University, 20-19, despite outstanding performances by Ray Hapes and Buster Poole.

The Miami experience helped Ole Miss see that it needed a sports

Bruiser Kinard (leading interference) rarely needed substitution and played 708 out of 720 minutes in 1935.

publicist. Gates talked Coach Harry Mehre into hiring him on a shared basis with the university's news bureau. Two events spurred Gates' desire for a full-time job: graduation and his 1937 marriage to Chris Murphree, an Ole Miss cheerleader whose Delta charm complemented Billy's career for 39 years.

Chris remembers Billy's first job with the athletic department was tenuous because of financial considerations. She recalls Coach Mehre telling Billy: "I can't afford to hire you, but I can't afford to do without you."

Mehre would not be disappointed. In Gates' first year of promotional efforts, halfback Parker Hall became the first of 21 All-Americans to receive national acclaim due to his hard work.

The prewar years were good to Ole Miss, but the war brought hard times and even the cancellation of the 1943 season. Gates became sports editor of the Baton Rouge Advocate in 1942. The next four years would be the only ones that he and Chris would spend away from Oxford.

When the war ended, Tommy Turner called Gates and told him Ole Miss was ready to start a big-time football program. He offered Gates his old job back.

"We had a family by then and Billy told him that he couldn't come

Coach Ed Walker's 1937 Ole Miss squad made history with the nation's first flight by a college team. They flew from Memphis to Philadelphia to play Temple.

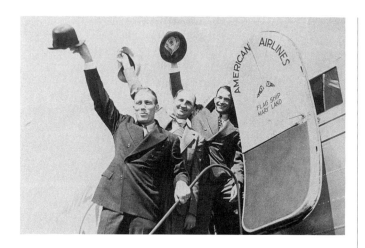

Bruiser Kinard, Coach Ed Walker and Ray Hapes

back for $100 a month," recalls Chris. "We did go back, but not for much more money."

Billy never cared much about money or its trappings. It's a good thing. Because his work was never fully appreciated, he went many years with little or no pay increase.

But he could laugh about money, too. He recalled for me one

afternoon in his office the day he told his father that he was marrying a girl from the Delta. "Son," his father said, "you've just married into long division."

Gates quickly became known as a dedicated, if not fanatic, statistician. He raised the practice of gathering statistics to an art form.

"They didn't keep records before Dad became the first SID," recalls son Bill, "so he went back and researched the games in old newspapers and recreated the stats from the clips."

"Stats were his forte," remembers attorney Clant Seay of Kosciusko, who worked as a spotter on the Ole Miss football network for 21 years. "The man was a master at it. He was ahead of his time."

His reputation for keeping and remembering Ole Miss football statistics often led to late-night phone calls to settle whiskey-induced bets, according to Bill. "It was nothing to

1938 All-America halfback Parker Hall (41)

get a call in the middle of the night and have somebody ask, 'What was the score of the 1949 Mississippi State game?' He could and would answer it and then the person might ask, 'Who scored the winning touchdown?' Daddy had a great memory. He could tell you not only who scored the winning touchdown, but he could generally describe the play for you."

His flair for statistics helped make his Rebel Guides famous.

"Those of us who grew up on those Rebel Guides could quote them like the Bible," said Seay.

"He set the trend nationally," marvels Langston Rogers, who now holds Gates' SID job. "You can see today his influence on media guides

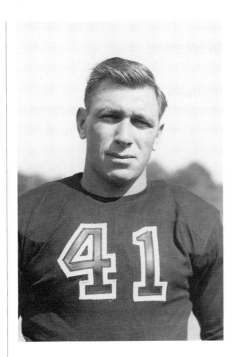

Parker Hall

Coach Ed Walker and his staff brought Ole Miss into national prominence: (l-r) Walker, Webb Burke, Tad Smith, Goat Hale and Chuck Smalling.

around the country."

Reading the Gates Rebel Guides is like sitting down to Sunday dinner at the Round Table in Mendenhall. So much on which to feast, impossible to digest it all at one time.

Take, for instance, the 1974 Rebel Guide, named the best in the country by the nation's sports information directors. The 180-page book—filled with color pictures, profiles, individual and cumulative statistics—also offers nuggets of trivia that could last a lifetime of winters.

What's the most points Ole Miss ever scored in a single games? (92 against West Tennessee Teachers in 1935.)

How many times has Ole Miss shut out the opposition? (103.)

Which Ole Miss team scored the most points in a season? (1959, 329 points: 45 touchdowns, 34 extra points, 5 field goals.)

Who scored the most points in a game? (Showboat Boykin, 42, against Mississippi State in 1951.)

Pick a stat, any stat, by game, season or career. Gates kept it and memorialized it in the Rebel Guides, the classic, enduring history books of Ole Miss football.

Billy Gates would drive a typical public relations executive crazy. He was not a back-slapper. He didn't suffer fools gladly. If journalists wrote or said something he didn't like, Gates would tell them directly.

Yet he was held in such high regard that he was named to virtually every Hall of Fame possible, state, regional and national, and his friends stretched across the country.

"He and mother were probably as well known in Mississippi as any couple who were not in politics," recalls son Bill. "It was hard to find a creek or a crevice in Mississippi where I was not Billy Gates, rather than Bill Gates. I had to leave Mississippi to be called Bill Gates."

Gates' achievements overshadowed his all-business personality.

"My forte was PR," recalls good friend Bob Hartley, the longtime SID at Mississippi State. "Billy was a great writer. He was dedicated to cranking out that mimeograph machine. Nobody could turn out copy better than Billy."

Gates gave newspapers a voluminous daily flow of stories during football season. In fact, a review of many daily and weekly sports sections in Mississippi would show that Gates-produced copy filled large parts of the sports sections. It was perfect for cost-conscious newspapers: well-written stories, accompanied by pictures, timely and, helpfully, totally free.

"They don't run handouts like that anymore," observes James (Bobo) Champion of Greenwood, who worked with Gates for four years and succeeded him at his death in 1976.

Hartley acknowledges that Gates' straight-forward personality caused some sportswriters to think

they were viewed as a necessary, distracting evil by Gates.

That may have been especially true following the idea of the SEC Skywriters Tour. To give its teams more visibility before the season, the conference chartered a plane and organized a barnstorming sportswriters tour of all the campuses. The junket may have provided a boon to many out-of-the-way SEC schools, but Gates had his own particular problems.

The last thing Johnny Vaught wanted to do as he was preparing for the upcoming season was spend a day with a planeload of sportswriters. Typically, Gates had to balance the desires of Vaught and the needs of the sportswriters.

"The sportswriters used to joke that Billy was probably sitting in Oxford hoping the plane would crash," Hartley said. "I knew better of course."

Friends of both Hartley and Gates knew the truth. Hartley had to use his considerable charm to attract press attention to Mississippi State. Gates stressed the facts and let the victories and winning ways speak for themselves. No one state ever had two better sports publicists.

The Gates persona prevailed in the press box on game day. He was driven to produce statistics and play-by-play descriptions that were accurate and fast. Woe be to the person who interfered with his objective.

The working press area of the new press box is named for Gates, a credit to his game-day regimen and sure-handed leadership in the press box that still cause me to look for him subconsciously nearly two decades after his death.

"He didn't like freeloaders in his press box," recalls Champion.

Nor did he like cheering fans in his press box, even if one was his son.

"I remember working in the press box for Dad helping keep statistics," recalls Bill. "Ole Miss scored on a big play and I leaned out the window and let out a big cheer. Dad planted his 9D shoe in my rear end, and I learned once and for all that cheerleaders belonged on the sidelines."

Sportswriting legends from around the South were familiar figures at the press box and the Gates home: Mississippi greats Lee Baker of the Jackson Daily News, Carl Walters and Wayne Thompson of The Clarion-Ledger, plus David Bloom of the Commercial Appeal, Fred Russell of the Nashville Banner and Tom Siler of the Knoxville News-Sentinel.

"Generally speaking, we won, so our house was a happy place after the games," said Bill. "Dad and the writers would trade a lot of stories and would get into endless discussions about which Ole Miss team was the best, which quarterback was the best."

Wife Chris says the post-game conversations at the house sometimes got animated.

"Billy and Tom Siler were eating spaghetti one night at the kitchen table," she recalls. "They got into this raging discussion about Coach Mehre vs. Coach Neyland. I hid the

butcher knives. When Tom left, he said he enjoyed the 'discussion' and smiled."

Appropriately, that's what I remember most about Billy Gates and Ole Miss football: smiles, thousands of smiles from his friends and associates as they recall a heyday of greatness.

For generations to come, we can pass on in rich detail the legends and stories of a remarkable half century—undeniably and forever the Gates Era.

Heroes in the Rain

Hapes goes over the top.

By Willie Morris

Heroes in the Rain

Willie Morris

T HE MOST precious consort of the writer, and the most elusive, is memory. Where does memory begin? How does old time itself shape it, render it, distill it, fuse the moments of childhood, so delicate and ethereal, into the hard retrospect of one's middle years? Memory is surely the most unfathomable of the human gifts.

The first college football game I ever saw... it came back to me in disconnected images–of the first real journey I ever made; of an immense stadium; of my father at the wheel of a big green DeSoto. Most of all, curiously, it was the rain which had recurred to me over the years, and the abiding moment my father wrapped me in his raincoat so I could watch the enigmatic proceedings far below while he withdrew for shelter.

First, then, the rain, and the drenched overcoat, and the black umbrellas all around me. And I was in the second grade there in Yazoo City, because I brought back a game program to my teacher, Mrs. Lois Page. That would have been 1941. And one of the teams was the Ole Miss Rebels, for I remembered that also, and Junie Hovious and Merle Hapes, the names Hovious and Hapes having inexplicably survived adolescence, young manhood, many loves and deaths, a few adulteries, several recessions, and three or four wars. And Memphis, that was the place, not easily forgotten when you were seven years old, good old Memphis, for I recalled too with remarkable clarity the enthralling bustle of it, its enormous buildings, its throngs of people, its clanging trolleys, the River from its bluffs.

With these imperishable clues, what game was it? On a yellowing schedule of the 1941 Ole Miss football season, I found three Saturday afternoon Ole Miss games in Memphis that year. I went to the Ole Miss library, giving these three dates to the pretty coed who worked in the microfilm collection, asking her to locate these issues of the Memphis Commercial Appeal. Just a moment, I said in afterthought—what I needed was the next day's issue which would have the Sunday football coverage. In a large filing cabinet she found the right containers. She inserted one of the rolls into a microfilm machine. The first date was November 23, 1941. The reproductions of aging newsprint

I could only reconstruct that long-ago contest as a sequence of dreams—long, towering kicks into the misty gray sky; strange men in striped shirts who blew whistles and little boys who dried off the footballs with towels; the players covered from head to foot with mud . . . grim phantoms struggling for their very lives.

Pep rally at The Peabody.

flickered before us on the screen.

There, suddenly, at the top of the very first page for November 23, an image leaped out at me. It was an eight-column photograph, the old-fashioned kind with a wide view of the football field and all the players in miniature with name tags under each figure. Superimposed on the photograph was a large headline:

OLE MISS 18, ARKANSAS 0

"Hold it there, miss," I said. I examined the picture more closely. "Is that mud?"

The girl too peered down. "It looks like mud to me."

"That's it, by God!" I exclaimed. "We got it on the first try. I'm there, somewhere up in those umbrellas." She looked up at me. I suspect she thought me somewhat deranged.

Why is it that the pages of old newspapers always make me sad? Is it their reminder of how transient all things are, of life ever so poignantly slipping by—of death itself? At home I studied the printouts of those pages. "Ole Miss Submerges Arkansas in Rain-Soaked Game"..."Sinkwich Runs Wild in Georgia Success"... "Vanderbilt 7, Alabama 0. Tennessee 20, Kentucky 7. Florida 14, Georgia Tech 7. Auburn 13, Villanova 0. Notre Dame 20, Southern Cal 18. Oklahoma 61, Marquette 14"..."Germans Launch Greatest Drive of War Against Moscow"..."How Near Are We to War?"

46

The "H-Boys," Junie Hovious and Merle Hapes

Coach Harry Mehre

These pages of the faithful Commercial Appeal opened the floodgates of remembrance for me, inundating me with those distant moments of my past. It was an eerie, nearly mystical feeling, as if some immemorial obstacle had abruptly dissolved and memories flowed out in waves, evoking for me in a rush the sights and sounds and smells of that childhood day fifty-one years ago.

I T WAS, indeed, the first genuine journey of my life. My father had promised me for weeks. I was lying in my front yard one night that fall, in the grass wet with dew, my head resting on a football as I looked up at the sky, when my father came out of the house and said, simply: "I'm going to take you to Memphis to see Ole Miss play."

My mother led me down to Ingram's Shoe Store on Main Street to buy me some new shoes. The day came to leave. I must have been enraptured by the spirit of the adventure, for I vividly recall retreating to the kennel in the backyard to pay a lengthy, ritualistic goodbye to our three hunting dogs, the affectionate companions of my early childhood. My father had been waiting in the car. Just before I got in, I asked if Tony, Sam, and Jimbo could go with us. His words now reverberate down the concourse of time. "They'd get lost in Memphis," he said.

Faint physical presences, wisps of perception, returned to me about this long drive north—stretches of gravel roads in the Delta, black crosses ever so often on the shoulders of the main highways which my father explained were where people had been killed in car accidents, the Negroes waving at us from the yards and porches of their unpainted shacks, the sea of dead cotton stalks under a dark and expansive sky, the unrelieved flatness of the black earth, my father peering through the windshield at the unhurried rain.

When we reached our destination we checked into the Chisca Hotel, because that is where we would always stay in Memphis, a rather weary and

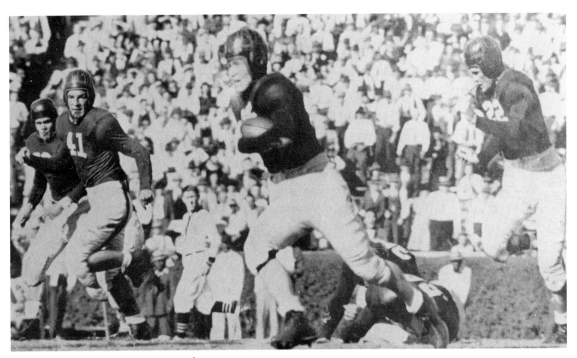

Junie Hovious enroute to a 96-yard punt return.

forlorn establishment off Union with pinball machines and cuspidors in the lobby; only later would I comprehend, of course, that we stayed in the Chisca because it was inexpensive. The big hotel room on one of the top floors was a wonderful revelation. It had the first bathroom shower I ever saw, and a view of the River all dusky in the rain, and of the bustling streets below. I absorbed Memphis in a trance. Is the world really this big? Do the lights stay on all night everywhere but in Yazoo? It must have been that first afternoon that my father took me by the hand and we walked up the broad boulevard with the trolleys moving back and forth to the Peabody Hotel. The grand lobby greeted me—ducks parading to a fountain, majestic chandeliers,

people drinking at tables encircled by large potted plants or waving flags and pennants with OLE MISS on them as they shouted and embraced and staggered madly about—and hovering over all this an aura of mystery and glitter that both frightened and titillated me.

The rain had stopped for a while the next morning; the traffic to Crump Stadium was heavy. The view of the stadium itself, once we had walked up a ramp inside, took my breath away—the immense field pooled with water; the row upon row of seats ascending, it seemed, to the murky heavens; the thousands of spectators with their umbrellas; the players of one team running about and exercising in all postures. A band was playing a song I later learned to know as "Dixie." Players from the other team raced onto the field and removed their red jackets to disclose unsoiled white jerseys and white pants. "That's Arkansas," my father said, although I must not have comprehended precisely what Arkansas was.*

I could only reconstruct that long-ago contest as a sequence of dreams—long, towering kicks into the misty gray sky; strange men in striped shirts who blew whistles and little boys who dried off the footballs with towels; the players covered from head to foot with mud, constantly slipping and falling or dropping the slippery ball, clawing and fighting one another in that ocean of mire until they seemed grim phantoms

---

*I still don't.

struggling for their very lives.

The Commercial Appeal provided me now with the names of those haphazard heroes. For Arkansas they were Pitts and Bynum and Sutton, Cato and Clark and Coats, Ramsay and Adams and Scarborough, Tibbitts and Delmonego and Forte. For Ole Miss they were Davidson and Kozel and Hazel, Wood and Britt and Flack, Thorsey and Bennett and Sam, Poole and Hovious and Hapes. The gallant Hovious and Hapes! Why do they remain with me to this day? I remember their dancing about in the mud, treacherous gallops for most of the length of the field, the crowd rising and cheering as they ran, so that Marcus Dupree's long runs for touchdowns forty years later would summon Hovious and Hapes for me.

Then, indelible as yesterday, the rain began again, descending in torrents. I felt gentle hands on my shoulders. My father was draping me in his raincoat, telling me to watch the game and not to go anywhere while he went down to a dry place.

Suddenly I was by myself in that prodigious stadium, surrounded by the exceptional sights and the unfamiliar people. A most unlikely figure I must have been there, a seven-year-old from the Mississippi Delta all alone in a soggy raincoat, the first time I had been so alone and so far from home. What could I have been thinking in that faraway moment? That the world is passingly strange? That it must be observed and

50

The 1941 freshman team, regarded as the best to date, included three future Hall of Famers: Charlie Conerly, Barney Poole, and Doug Kenna, but war would soon replace football.

remembered? That there is sadness in exuberance? Or was I merely frightened again, as I had been in the lobby of the Peabody? Recognition failed me anew on such august scrutinies. I only recall the cluster of girls in white boots and raincaps sitting down the way, the boisterous strangers next to me passing a bottle among themselves and drinking from it in long gulps, the sounds of the band and the yells of "Hotty, Toddy!", the laughter when one of the men in striped shirts was run over by a player and skidded for yards in the mud, the jubilant chant of "Hovious, Hovious!" when the little silhouette abruptly moved and darted through the other phantoms trying to wrestle him to the earth— and, all about me as I gazed behind me to see if I could find my father, the eternal Southern rain.

Not too long ago I sought out Junie Hovious, who was retired now from coaching football at Ole Miss. "It's funny. I don't remember a thing about that game. Maybe I'm just gettin' old. Or maybe I only remember the close ones."

Billy Sam, the Rebel right half-back, was killed on the beaches of Saipan, Hovious remembered. Larry Hazel, the left tackle, perished when his parachute failed to open in flight training in Pensacola. He stays in touch with a few of the others from that day. "Some have been in real bad health," he said. "Some have retired. Some I haven't heard head or tails of. Some I'm not sure are alive or dead."

One thing I had not forgotten of the morning after the game when my father and I were about to leave. Nothing would deny me my vibrant memory of actually thanking our hotel room for showing me such a good time, of saying farewell to it and telling it I would return to it someday.

Two weeks later to the day was December 7, 1941. When the news came and was explained to me, I went to the kennel in the backyard. Sitting among Tony, Sam, and Jimbo as they gave me moist licks on the face, I began to cry, tears surely as torrential as the Memphis rain; the Japs were coming to Mississippi.

The Golden Age

By William Winter

The Golden Age

William Winter

$\mathbb{M}$ AN AND BOY I have been present at most of the
football games that Ole Miss has played over the
last fifty years. My first one was the 1939 contest with St.
Louis University, which the Rebels won 42 to 0. The stars
that afternoon before a homecoming crowd of 5,500 were
the "H-Boys," Junie Hovious and Merle Hapes, and All-
SEC end Jesse Ward. It was the last game that Ward ever
played. He would be killed in a tragic automobile wreck later
that evening.

There have been so many memorable events and individu-
als involving Ole Miss football since that long-ago day that it
is difficult to single out one player or one game. There was, of
course the incomparable Archie Manning who became the
most talked-about and exciting player ever to wear the Red and
Blue. There was Jake Gibbs from my hometown of Grenada,
under whose almost flawless quarterbacking the Rebels lost
only one game in two years–that haunting Halloween shootout in Tiger Stadium in 1959. But we got that one back in
the Sugar Bowl two months later 21 to 0.

Who can ever forget that only perfect record season of
1962, when Glynn Griffing led Ole Miss to national acclaim
at a time when we were not faring well otherwise? Who
among us who were there will ever forget beating mighty
Maryland in 1952 or Notre Dame in 1977 or Texas in the
Sugar Bowl.

Even if there had been no other games on the schedule
the series with Mississippi State would have provided excitement enough. It is still painful for me to recall that game
in Oxford a week before Pearl Harbor when for the only
time in history we played each other for the championship of
the SEC, and the underdog Bulldogs won 6 to 0. There are
many other more satisfying memories, though, including
the incredible "divine wind" game of 1983 and most recently the fabulous goal line stand for eleven downs in the season just ended.

But, if I were compelled to single out one game and one
player that stand out for me above all others for sheer drama

*What will stand
out perhaps above
all else about that
epic season
happened off the
field. It was a
simple affirmation
of integrity by the
leadership of the
University.*

Charlie Conerly, All-America halfback (1947)

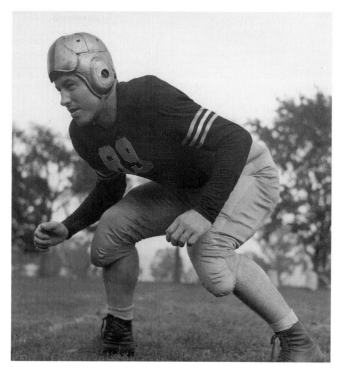

Barney Poole, All-America end (1947)

and excitement, I would have to go back to a November evening in 1947. The setting not surprisingly was Tiger Stadium. This was the game that would lead to Ole Miss's first SEC title. LSU was a heavy favorite, led by the great Y. A. Tittle. However, Ole Miss had a halfback of its own—a fellow from Clarksdale by the name of Conerly. Both Tittle and Conerly would later quarterback the New York Giants to outstanding seasons in the NFL.

In this game the lead surged back and forth all night. It was finally Conerly and the Rebels who prevailed 20 to 18 in a contest that the late Walter Stewart of the Memphis Commercial Appeal described as follows: "They didn't even carry out the heart failures. They just stood on them in order to see more clearly." Charlie Conerly ran for all three Ole Miss touchdowns. He would go on to be All-American and All-Pro.

That was the climactic game in a season that marked the beginning of the Vaught era—the golden age of Ole Miss football.

It had begun surprisingly enough in the season's opening game at Hemingway Stadium where the Rebels upset Bear Bryant's Kentucky Wildcats 14 to 7. Each game thereafter was a drama-filled series of Conerly to Barney Poole heroics with a controversial loss to Vanderbilt the only conference setback. A season-ending wipe-out of Mississippi State 33 to 14 was almost anticlimactic.

Coach John Howard Vaught: Football Writers National Championship (1960), six SEC titles, 18 bowl games, SEC Coach of the Year in 1947 and 1962.

John Vaught's staff, which molded a championship team in 1947, were (l-r, kneeling) Wesley "Doc" Knight, John "Hurry" Cain, Junie Hovious, Tom Swayze; (standing) Bruiser Kinard, Jim Watley, Vaught, Wobble Davidson and Buster Poole.

In addition to the first SEC title, two All-Americans, and John Vaught's spectacular inaugural, what will stand out perhaps above all else about that epic season happened off the field. It was a simple affirmation of integrity by the leadership of the University. In the summer before the season began Ole Miss, which had won all of two games the year before, signed an agreement to play in the newly-created Delta Bowl in Memphis on New Year's Day. No one in his wildest dreams envisioned a conference championship and an invitation to the Sugar or the Orange Bowl.

At season's end the Delta Bowl seemed a small reward for so successful a team. There were suggestions that the contract be ignored. Someone asked Dean James Warsaw Bell, the chairman of the Athletic Committee, about it.

"We are bound by honor to play in Memphis, and we will play in Memphis," the old Dean said. "Taking another bid would besmirch the name of Ole Miss, and our good name is worth more than anything I know of. We might make more money somewhere else, but it would only be money — and not quite clean."

And play in Memphis we did.

The starting team for the 1947 S.E.C. champions (l-r): Everette Harper, re; Doug Hamley, rt; Jim Crawford, rg; Dave Bridgers, c; Bernard Blackwell, lg; Bill Erickson, lt; Barney Poole, le; (backs) Farley Salmon, rhb; Red Jenkins, fb; Buck Buchanan, qb; and Charlie Conerly, captain, lhb (not pictured, Buddy Bowen, qb).

On a frozen field in 30-degree weather with a 35-mile an hour wind blowing out of the west, Conerly threw for two touchdowns in the final quarter to beat Coach Vaught's alma mater, Texas Christian University, 13 to 9. That night the Rebel star was named the nation's "Player of the Year." That was the year that set the stage for the many great seasons that were to follow.

Line Coach Bruiser Kinard with tackles Doug Hamley and Roland Dale. (Note Stadium construction in background.)

Confessions of a
Drum Major

By James A. Autry

Confessions of a Drum Major

IF YOU think playing football is a rough endeavor at Ole Miss, you ought to try wearing tight britches and a tall fuzzy hat and leading the Rebel Band in front of 50,000 screaming people who want you to get the hell off the field so the game can begin.

Now that's what I call high risk.

When Band Director Lyle Babcock asked me to be drum major during my senior year, 1954-55, he sweetened his request with the offer of $100 a month during the football season. I believe it was called something like a work scholarship.

In those days, when some of my fellow students were financing their educations with everything from never-ending poker games in Girard Hall to providing the visiting alums with special beverages brought in from Memphis for football weekends, I figured that playing drum major for $100 a month would be the easiest money I ever made. I was on a band scholarship and had to be there anyway. Why not just be out in front?

Somehow my enthusiasm for the money distracted me from the realization that I also would have to wear the tight pants and the tall fuzzy hat.

I know football is a rough game, but no All-American tackle ever had to march for an hour in a Sugar Bowl parade, knowing that in every block at least one kid was going to try to knock off his hat with a rock. There were times the crowd gave me great applause for my innovative strutting when all I was doing was dodging rocks.

The tight pants had special perils as well. First there were the snide comments from men all along the way. Most of them are unprintable.

Then there was the majorette—who in this space shall remain nameless—who took a strange sadistic pleasure in trying to make herself especially alluring as we waited to march or to go on the field for the halftime show. The results of her flirting are also unprintable; suffice it to say that my costume seemed to shrink.

James A. Autry

I know football is a rough game, but no All-America tackle ever had to march for an hour in a Sugar Bowl parade, knowing that in every block at least one kid was going to try to knock off his hat with a rock.

Ole Miss band led by a predecessor of James Autry, who was drum major in 1954.

This is not say that the machinations of the majorette were the only contact sport involved in drum-majoring. To the contrary, we in the band regularly had our contact with the football players themselves.

There were several times when the halftime show was still in progress as the teams came back from the locker rooms. There we were, still on the field, marching and playing our hearts out, when suddenly we would be invaded by gigantic men in colorful costumes who had just spent the past fifteen minutes being told they were not mean enough.

When they came on the field, they were not smiling and they were not enjoying the music. They had been told to knock down anyone wearing a uniform different from theirs. Apparently they thought this included the band.

I found myself in the turf only once, however, probably because of the footwork I had developed dodging rocks.

But it was not all peril by any means. I confess also that there is no more rewarding feeling than leading the Rebel Band onto the field at halftime and hearing the faithful fans roar with approval as we did our stuff.

There is a great deal to be said for being part of the pageantry that makes up the Ole Miss football experience, and there are times even now, almost 40 years later, when I see a game and think, "I don't know how all the other former drum majors feel, but I'd do it all again—fuzzy hat, tight britches, majorettes, rocks, and all."

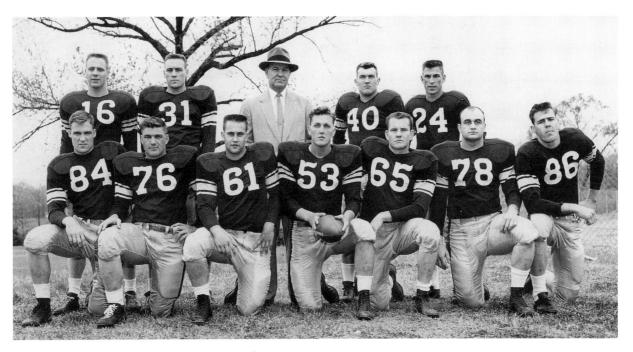

The 1953 Rebel team* included a future Ole Miss head coach, halfback Billy Kinard (31): (kneeling, l-r)
Buddy Harbin, Archie Shepherd, Rodgers Brashier, Bobby McKinney, Raymond James, Richard Weiss,
Billy Yelverton; (back row) Houston Patton, Kinard, Vaught, Paige Cothren, Jimmy Patton.

Rebel cheerleaders in 1954: (from left) Barney Eaton, Jimmy Walkner, Carl
Downing, Charles Davis; (second row) Shirley Wagner, Laura Cloud, Kay
Horton and Shirley Walne.

*If these men had run over the band after halftime, James Autry might not be alive to tell about it.

Violet Mulvenna, National Baton
Champion

Kristi Lynn Addis, Miss Teen USA 1987

66

WALT MIXON

A Dream of
the Big Contender

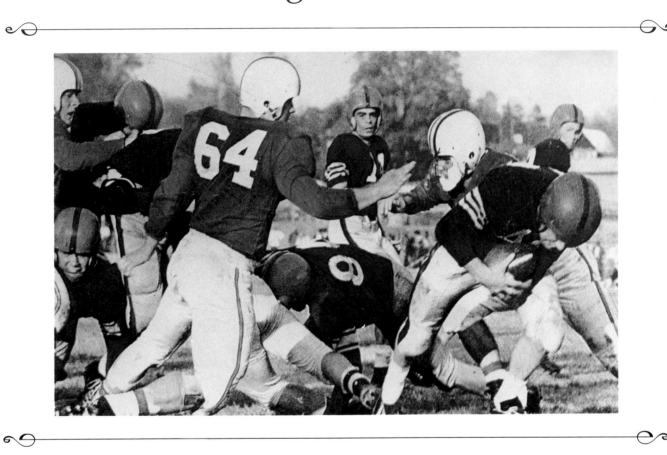

By Barry Hannah

A Dream of
the Big Contender

Talking of others, old men talk about themselves, studying their image in vanished mirrors."
> —John LeCarre, in "The Honourable Schoolboy"

Barry Hannah

S AMUEL BECKETT, who revealed no apparent hope in his Nobel-worthy prose and drama, could not even get raretied about love itself. "No, no love. Only bodies." The most excited he ever got was about cricket, of which he was a lifelong zealot. In his youth in Ireland he was an accomplished player. Albert Camus, another Nobel recipient, told us he learned everything he ever knew about ethics from playing sports in Algeria. What's going on here? Are our best minds subsidizing every dreary jock we've passed by?

Does our football, too drenched by cliches and bad writing for a hundred years now, really need another essay? No, though I jump in, gladly. It does not need the commendations of literary lions, or the approval of bookish sissies. For many of us it's simply like oxygen: sometimes you need it. For me and many pals, it is deep and real and necessary—one of the truly good passions, even as the players increase in size and speed by the month, and recede, or exceed, into the clouds of improbable myth like the Greeks worshipped, away from merely average us.

Not a host, but only two or three dreams lead us through a lifetime, it seems to me. They are likely to start about the time real consciousness bangs on your head. For me it was something at ten years old I saw on the football field at Hemingway Stadium after a grass-wrecking game in the fifties. A big Rebel player was just standing there easy, about the forty yard line, one hand on his helmet and the other engaged in the fingers of a doting and proud Ole Miss cheerleader. He was chatting happily maybe a little natural swagger to him with some doting and proud parents, maybe hers. His smile and big shoulders just staggered me. Here was a merry god, and good things like that cheerleader and the fawning adults were his just desserts. He was in red, blue and gray, colors that pulsed to me across the air and green. He was a collection of all

He was in red, blue and gray, colors that pulsed to me across the air and green. He was a collection of all American history, the best stuff . . his jersey and pants streaked by grass and dirt, his friendly eyes underscored by black smears so he could see to fight in the sun.

Above: Kline
Gilbert, All-
America Tackle
(1952)

Right: In 1951
halfback A.L.
"Showboat"
Boykin scored a
record seven
touchdowns
against Mississippi
State.

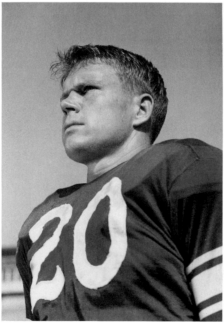

American history, the best stuff, and nobody deserved his leisure like that man did at the moment, with his jersey and pants streaked by grass and dirt, his friendly eyes underscored by black smears so he could see to fight in the sun. Behind his back you might sense Adolph Hitler torn to bits by him and his mates, the big shy fellow claiming Aw shucks, it wasn't that much to it. I don't recall now that team Ole Miss had just played, maybe Tulane in their fruity strange colors like Ireland. And I don't know who the player was, and gave scant attention to his babe—no time for her, sorry, it was the fifties and the commie threat was on us—but the smiling face, the sweat in his hair, with the sun about gone and leaving us colder, was a compound of all you wanted to be as a man.

The dream shot through me, and broke my heart when I wound up a mere fan, trumpet-player and tennis wimp. Football was in the family blood. My brother, eleven years older, was star end at Mississippi College. My uncle, who gave his life flying against Rommel in Africa, had been an instant stud at Mississippi Southern, having never even played the game in high school. My pa was beside me in a shrine of his own that afternoon. He spoke reverently of Coach Johnny Vaught until the day he died at age 87. He was quick to introduce me to Rebel football, abiding by the holy rite of initiation charged to University of Mississippi

The 1959 Rebels, named SEC Team-of-the-Decade by the Associated Press, were (l-r, first row) Cowboy Woodruff, Bobby Crespino, Jimmy Champion, Jimmy Hall, George Blair, Doug Elmore, Billy Brewer, Jake Gibbs, Bobby Ray Franklin; (second row) Jimmy Robinson, Frank Halbert, Art Doty, Billy Ray Adams, Charlie Flowers, James Anderson, Dewey Partridge, Reggie Robertson, Billy Ray Jones, Fred Lentjes; (third row) Allen Green, Ken Kirk, Warner Alford, Bill Basham, Charles Kempinska, Marvin Terrell, Shedd Roberson, Wayne Terry Lamar, Richard Price, John Mitchell, Jerry Brown; (fourth row) Rush McKay, Robert Khayat, Bob Benton, Bobby Owens, Joe Robertson, Jerry Daniels, Johnny Brewer, Ralph Smith, Bernie Regan, Warren Ball, Gibbs Goodwin and Larry Grantham.

Coach Vaught with quarterbacks Billy Brewer and Bobby Ray Franklin

73

Above: Fullback
Charlie Flowers
(41) was co-cap-
tain of the 1959
"Dream Team."

Jackie Simpson,
All-America
guard (1957)

fathers—though I became only a
sort of bothered nothing, a worm,
maybe even seen in the library, vol-
untarily, sometimes—snarling, envi-
ous. This was the fifties. Football
was church and flag both.

More and more, the fifties are
becoming poignant to me, for after
all they gave me my lifetime dreams.
There was less Eisenhower-tempered
conformity than is commonly supposed, and more individuality. Folks
created their own play more then.
More utterly loose genius abounded,
making current wildness appear
rather a mannerism, compared.
Mose Allison, dismissed for herbal
pioneering at Ole Miss, I understand, was well into his very unwhite
piano jazz, and was our first cult figure when we heard his records in the
early sixties. V. P. Ferguson wired
up a PA system in some quad of
dorms here, and woke everybody at
daybreak with the screaming
announcement "Ladies and gentlemen, I give you...the sun!"
McCarthy paranoia had its uses for
the very young. We imagined a
neighborhood fiend called Red Top
who besieged Clinton, Mississippi
relentlessly and invisibly. He left
tragic symbols of wicked commie
schemes here and there, and sometimes made commie zombies out of
odd, private old people we whispered
about, à la "Invasion of the Body"
Snatchers—a paradigm of fifties
suspicion we hadn't even seen yet.
It was our duty to report and resist,
in our tiny patriot ways, even maybe
tear off the flower from some dis-
agreeable hermit's lawn so that he

would know. Yes, he would know that we knew. The hovering of the A-and H-bombs over the community provided a field day for the preachers, who had their Apocalypse handy. There was much more fire and brimstone from the pulpit in those days, scaring the hell out of the young, like me, who walked the Baptist aisles five or six times rededicating my life, so many times that my mother, no slack church lady herself, was embarrassed and pulled me aside for quiet advice of her own. I see some disoriented old preachers still about who never recovered from the fact the bombs never fell (on us, anyway).

In my science class, the football coach, a Third Army vet, told us we had seen nothing until we saw a man burning alive in a tank. Later, on the field, he proceeded to coach in the old style where the premise is that you were, every one of you, vile unworthy grubs, guilty of every weakening habit when you were out of his sight. I was a fair quarterback until tenth grade, when I began growing smaller and smaller. Or something. I gave myself over to trumpet, a baleful decision for the second-rate, I felt then. Aristocracy—the only one we had in town—was in football. The only true swagger was in football. The better girls attended...football. Their smiles, wearing their beaux' letter jackets, could make a nerd tremble with envy. Come to think of it, the good fifties gave us the proto-nerd, without whom much of our delicious cruelty might have no object. Nowadays, closet nerds, liberated by drink, can be seen throwing ice and toilet paper and bot-

Eddie Crawford, halfback (1956)

Warner Alford, guard, co-captain of the 1960 National Champions.

75

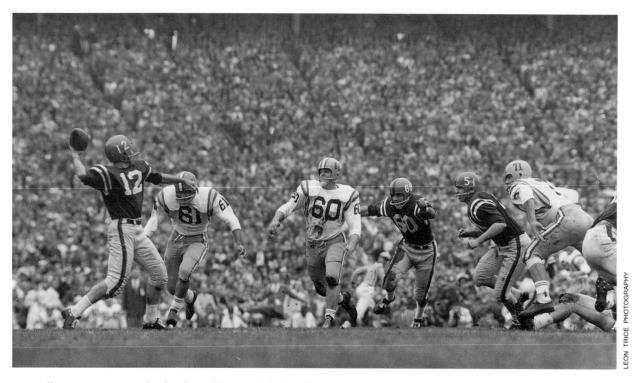

LEON TRICE PHOTOGRAPHY

All-America Quarterback Jake Gibbs (12) led the Rebels to a 21-0 rematch victory over LSU in the 1960 Sugar Bowl.

tles at the opposing bench with impunity from their lonely ardent crowd.

In the fifties we had the privilege of beholding the Teams of the Decade, then Century, at Ole Miss, who ranked first in the nation—a team from a student body of around 4000, I think, in the poorest state in the union.

Head Coach Billy Brewer, whose sanity in both victory and defeat has always impressed me, has recently noted that none of these football Rebels could have made the modern 1992 team: too slow; himself, a vivid star then, included. But they did have something metaphysical about them under Johnny Vaught. I play tennis with a fellow from the fifties teams. A good five years older than I (serious about it since 1959, snarling), and much heavier, with big football legs under him, and frequently blowing out the detritus of last night's atomic party, James Hall—without the grandest strokes, either—won't quit running, won't give up, and get this: he won't drink water. That was probably what sissies did in the fifties, need fluid. According to Hall, the fifties Rebels could play if only one leg was broken, and drank their own sweat, if water was that urgent. Their models came from gravely wounded Marines on Tarawa and Iwo Jima, invoked by "Contact" Coach Wobble Davidson and approved by the Good Commander Vaught.

You still see aged Rebel adults, bemused like those old preachers, dreaming of those days when men were men—all white men then, alas—and tiny Ole Miss was the theater of national myth. Most of these old men I've met, by the way, are knightly gentlemen with a kindness and honesty that come to those who've had a touch of glory. They are generous, loyal through the worst, and sweetly pleased at the rewriting of myth by the '92 Ole Miss defense, a team at the end of the season so good, we fans—nerds, would-bes, wannabes (wildly pedantic about the game), and just prideful Mississippians with our knockout dates (who can now think and do and have honorable jobs, our long-way babies)—might sense we can never see such champions

again. But thanks, Lord of Football. Our memory has sack and stomp bruises all over it, and we smile like the big guys in the big bad red and blue. You've driven us baba. Years ago Dean Wells, Faulkner's scrappy niece and fellow South End Zone Rowdy, told me she wanted to be Gator Bennett. The work of Cassius Ware, Dewayne Dotson, Chad Brown, Artis Ford, et. al., brought tears to my fetching wife Susan's eyes this season. What great boys, what courageous smart men! she cried. Beside her, I myself, rowdy and deep like only a never-made-it can be, wept openly as if we were the good side and Vicksburg had been retaken. Eleven times, maroon State was inside our ten yard line in the last minutes. Rally, lads, into the breech once again. One foot from the goal at one tragic moment, the poor Bullies were knocked back four yards and had to hand over the ball. Coach Brewer, whose stature is steadily and deservedly growing in this hard league, said he'd never seen anything like it. It was just impossible.

But it all started in the good fifties for me.

My pa brought me up to Oxford with his friends, who included an ex-player for Ole Miss named Solly Crain, our school principal. He must have played in the twenties, a decade whose photographs catch men in meager pads and cross-banded leather dufus helmets. The men seem almost valiant in bad taste, somehow angry and happy at the same time; memories

77

of the vanquished Kaiser Bill, maybe, in their heads. They seem to be in immediate pain, but rather enjoying it. The very air seems grayer and grim, like England, or was this just the old cameras? In fact the men in the photos seem vaguely retarded, as if on a leash just broken off the wall of an institution. It was hard to imagine Mr. Crain, merry, mean and crouched like that, running riot on the turf, although he was a dread figure in the halls in those days when a principal might listen to your problem for a while, then beat you. I never spoke one word to him. Still, he was my pa's friend. Already you got the feeling of Oxford as a mecca, with happy but serious pilgrims attending, as we passed in a line of cars through the little towns of Duck Hill and Water Valley.

Oxford was woodsier and more evergreenly then. I recall all South Lamar, with its whopping Victorian manses, coming at me like Gone With the Wind. This was a whole other country. It stuck in my boy heart, this beauty, like my first kiss, which I don't even remember. All was spread out in wide light plumpfull of yellow, orange, red and purple leaves, the pavement thick with them like a carpet from Turkey; the grass was beige like a cheerleader's cheeks.

In the stadium I remember a man in red and blue breaking free, the sudden eruption of our crowd, great Sousa congratulations from the band, and waving through it all the smell of roasted peanuts and good whiskey; a big fall chill full of spices, the well-decked women all looking like June Allyson, smelling like warm roses and other things I would learn quickly to love. Preparation for heaven, but not quite the full vision yet. Ole Miss won, and we were on the field itself among the jubilant fans and the very warriors for our side. That's when I saw the big fellow, his cheerleader alongside—all tender and worshipful—and the adults who couldn't get enough of him. Him shrugging, lowering his head in modesty, with his eyes painted black for battle. Back in the heavy and slow fifties, here was the aristocrat of my time within touching distance. Here was all the astronaut I needed. Here was life at its brave absolute best. Here was the national contender, one of an uninterrupted phalanx of Gippers, the Ole Miss Rebels. I'd already memorized their wonderful rakish cheer, "Hotty Toddy!" and later whispered it around the home, caressing *hell* and *damn* as only an oppressed Baptist child can.

Now, of course, there is a line of moderation about football past which the poetry really becomes bad and fanatic, and if you pass it you go to hell and have to stand in a field of broken glass among Caligula, Nero, Stalin and Idi Amin, where the bubbling Welk band never quits, and you are tortured to admit there really was no Saint Archie or Chad of Nazareth. They were a forced illusion shaped by sad men without a life of their own. And you beg forgiveness for your neglect of the poor, the sick and the heathen. There were much worthier loves to get charged about, you admit, and you have lent yourself to a childish thing. The A-bomb was really you yourself, there in your pathetic red and blue outfit, a program in your hands, peanut grime on your lip, still hoarse—the whimper not the bang—at eighty. But yet, Lord: How can it all have felt so good, watching our Big Contenders? Just a little relief from the rutted small-town ennuis, money, the rent, maybe? Just a piece of the grand light, the cheers that actually move the air around.

I didn't even go to Ole Miss. No, I was a Choctaw, then a loathsome Razorback, and spent twenty years out of the state, intending never to come back, for various personal reasons. I get asked in interviews a lot why I came and settled in Oxford. They already know the answer, since I'm a fiction writer. It was Faulkner, wasn't it? It was the ghost of Faulkner. They've practically written it down, and I nod: Yeah, Faulkner, our own Nobel guy. The ghost of Faulkner.

But it's a lie. It was, of course, that old dream kicking around, then finally grabbing me by the neck. That champion, lowering his head in modesty, Mississippi turf all over him, eyes painted black for battle. That old contender in red and blue. I wonder who he was, and I surely do wish him well.

The Return

By John Grisham

The Return

M
Y CHILDHOOD was spent in various small towns throughout the Deep South, most of them in Arkansas. In the summer of 1966, my parents moved to Ripley, Mississippi, for one year, and because my new Scoutmaster there was a rabid Rebel fan, I found myself one beautiful autumn afternoon sitting in the stands at Hemingway Stadium. My entire troop was there, all dressed nattily in green, all waving flags and yelling at the field. I was eleven, and it was my first college football game. In fact, it was my first trip to Oxford, a town I would much later adore and call home.

The opponent was Southern Mississippi, a team which had never beaten Ole Miss before 1966. Our seats were on the Southern side, near the north end zone. Ole Miss trailed for three quarters, and as the time slipped away the Southern fans smelled victory and grew much rowdier. The fourth quarter started with Ole Miss trailing by a touchdown, 7-0. An upset was looming.

For a sixth-grader, I had excellent speed and quick feet, talents that would mysteriously disappear in high school. And I loved football. Gale Sayers of the Bears was my hero, and I lived for the footage of him spinning and cutting for eighty yards, breaking tackles and leaping bodies until he found the promised land. This was long before linebackers with 4.6 speed, and broken-field running was still an art form. I dreamed of taking punts and kickoffs, just like Gale Sayers, then slicing through walls of tacklers, zigzagging across the field with my blinding speed as the crowds screamed deliriously for more.

It never happened, of course. But I was a boy, and I had a vivid imagination.

The fourth quarter was half-gone when Southern punted from deep in its own territory. The ball bounced somewhere around midfield, and for a second seemed to be just another harmless punt. But the Rebel return man, Doug Cunningham, No. 22, sprang from nowhere, took the ball, and was immediately surrounded by white jerseys. He was hit, broke a tackle,

MARION VANCE

John Grisham

Doug Cunningham crossed the goal line all alone . . . and nonchalantly flipped the ball to the official. No bodily gyrations. No ripping off his helmet so the world could see him. No strutting or somersaults. Just a casual little lateral of the ball, as if he'd been in the end zone before.

83

Above: Tailback Doug Cunningham, 1966 co-captain

Right: The author, "School Days," Ripley Elementary, 1966-67.

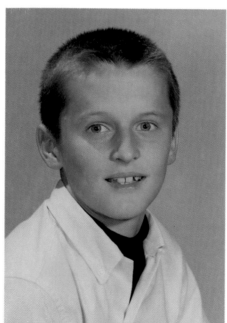

hit again, shook himself free, darted one way then the other, and suddenly emerged from the pile of humanity with his legs pumping, his knees high in the air, his hips twisting, and two blockers in front of him. The crowd erupted.

Cunningham cut to the sideline in front of us, and hit the afterburners. For a few brief seconds, time that is still frozen in my memory, Doug Cunningham galloped toward the north end zone with unmatched speed, and crossed the goal line all alone. He circled by a fence, long since removed, and nonchalantly flipped the ball to the official. No bodily gyrations. No ripping off his helmet so the world could see him. No showy prayer. No strutting or somersaults. Just a casual little lateral of the ball, as if he'd been in the end zone before.

THREE minutes later, he scored again, and Ole Miss won 14-7.

Though I can't testify from personal experience, I suspect there are few moments in life as exhilarating as running a long touchdown while thousands scream and cheerleaders turn flips. Nailing a three pointer at the buzzer must rank pretty high. (Never happened to me.) Stepping into a high, hard fastball and watching it disappear over the centerfield wall is probably a real charge. (I wouldn't know.) But football has the element of danger—of large, angry, inspired enemies seeking desperately to remove your head, of muscular bod-

Cunningham enroute to a 57-yard punt return.

Ole Miss backfield coach Junie Hovious and 1962 quarterbacks Glynn Griffing (15), Perry Lee Dunn (10), Bobby Boyd (16) and Jim Weatherly (12).

Kenny Dill, All-America center (1963)

ies flying through the air, of people shrieking in pain. It must be thrilling to take the ball and dash and dart through such mayhem.

Anyway, the game ended and we left Hemingway. I worked my way through the crowd, cutting here, spinning there, bouncing off would-be-tacklers, legs pumping high, hips twisting, just like Doug Cunningham. For weeks and months afterwards, in countless sandlot and playground games, I fielded punts and kickoffs, faked one way then another, and occasionally hit the sideline, just like Doug Cunningham.

One day, I was certain, I would hear the roar of the crowd, and I would watch the scoreboard record my deeds.

Such are the dreams of boys.

Stan Hindman (67), 1965 All-America guard, and Bobby Robinson, guard and 1964 co-captain

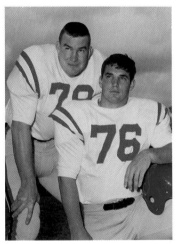

Eight players signed pro contracts in 1965: (front, l-r) tackle Jim Harvey, end John Maddox, guard Stan Hindman, tackle Tommy Lucas; (back row) wingback Dave Wells, halfback Billy Clay, quarterback Jimmy Heidel, tailback Mike Dennis.

1967 All-America tackle Jim Urbanek (left) and Dan Sartin.

1960 SEC champions and winners of the Grantland Rice Award given to the Number One team in the nation.

Shootout at Legion Field

By Billy Watkins

Shootout at Legion Field

ARCHIE MANNING wanted to try something different. He recalled how former Ole Miss teammate Bill "Indian" Matthews used to play without socks, his feet and ankles covered only with tape.

So three hours before Ole Miss would play Alabama in the first prime-time national telecast of a college football game — Oct. 4, 1969, at Birmingham's Legion Field — Doc Knight, the longtime Rebel trainer, carefully decorated Archie's feet with adhesive "socks."

First thing Archie noticed was the pain. "I was miserable," he recalls. "The tape was cutting into my feet...I could barely walk." But Ole Miss had lost to Kentucky 10-9 the week before, and, although Archie wasn't the superstitious type, he was determined to try something new.

With no socks and aching feet, Archie Manning touched all of us. We touched him right back by making him a bonafide national hero.

The question wasn't "Archie Who?" but "Archie Where?" Alabama never found him. He ran and passed for 540 total yards, scored three touchdowns, set seven records and proved that big-time college football indeed had a place on national television.

He also lost by a point. Alabama 33, Ole Miss 32.

There is something especially dramatic about the hero losing the girl at the end. Archie Manning spat in the eye of Bear Bryant's defense, brought the Rebels from behind four times — twice in the fourth quarter — and had them moving when time ran out. You cried right along with Archie as he walked off Legion Field, proud but beaten.

"That game made me," Archie says. "I went through my sophomore season and got some good coverage in the Southeast. But the one that put me in the national picture was that game."

Archie's statistics: 15 rushes for 104 yards, including scrambles of 30, 17, 16, 17 and 21 yards; 52 passes, 33 completions, 436 yards, 2 touchdowns, 1 interception.

Billy Watkins

"I looked up at the referee and called timeout, and he looked me square in the eye and did nothing. I watched the clock and with each second that ticked off I kept getting this feeling that all was lost. I know you shouldn't get those feelings about a football game, but we had been in combat for hours."
—Floyd Franks

And he lost. By one point. On a missed extra-point kick.

"When I went to Viet Nam on a USO trip in 1973, ninety percent of the soldiers I met over there, that game is what they talked about," Archie says. "Through the years, the people I meet around the country, that's what they remember. It's been 24 years — 24 years — but I don't go many weeks without somebody bringing up that game.

"Now when I go to Alabama, that's all they talk about. But they get the score mixed up. 'Was it 44-43? 31-30? 38-37?' And they get the quarterbacks mixed up. 'Wasn't that you and Stabler? You and Namath?' Poor Scott gets forgotten sometimes."

Not in Mississippi. Scott Hunter is forever remembered as the guy who completed 22 of 29 passes for 300 yards. One touchdown, no interceptions.

And Mississippians can't forget the score: 33-32.

ABC TELEVISION was only in its fourth season of broadcasting college football then.

"We were actually promoting it as much as telecasting it," says Chris Schenkel, the veteran announcer who worked the 33-32 game along with Bud Wilkinson and Bill Flemming. "That's why I'd always say that line that I'm still mimicked about. 'What a way to spend a Saturday afternoon. All the color and pageantry that is college football.'"

That one game, in prime time for all the nation to see, did more for college football than the previous three seasons combined, according to Schenkel.

"Without question, that game got us going," says Schenkel. "Oh, God, if you could write a script...It was a thriller between two teams that have helped build the history of college football since Day 1."

Schenkel, who has broadcast more than 700 college and professional football games, says it was "the epitome of college football" and he calls it "one of the top two or three games I've done."

Ole Miss-Alabama was an emotional game for Schenkel. "I've always had a thing about Ole Miss," he says. "Back when I used to do the (New York) Giant games, half the roster was players from Ole Miss. Charlie Conerly, all the Pooles, Jimmy Patton, the best safety there ever was. Mention Ole Miss, and my lights would go on.

"And I loved Coach (Johnny) Vaught. He would always give us Ole Miss's game plan. But we were also friends with Bear Bryant. Every time we'd do an Alabama game he'd have dinner with Bud and me the night before."

Schenkel remembers that night in Birmingham this way: "Legion Field was a sea of red...the lights were hotter than hell...it was a sellout (62,858)...the press box at Legion Field was so high up, you loved it when one guy stood out, and Archie was easy to pick out because he was taller (6-foot-3) than everybody else. And he was so damn flamboyant."

THE BIRMINGHAM NEWS

Scott Hunter

ESIDES the all-for-nothing performance by Archie, there is another fact about the game that shreds Mississippians' insides: two boys from Meridian, both wide receivers, helped lead Alabama to victory.

George Ranager, a lanky junior who had starred with Archie in the 1967 Mississippi High School All-Star game, caught 3 passes for 68 yards, including the game-winner on fourth-and-10 with 3:42 left. Ranager was also the Tide's leading rusher with 74 yards on 4 carries.

David Bailey, a sophomore making only his third collegiate start, caught 9 passes for 115 yards. Three of his catches were in crucial third-down situations.

They signed with Alabama for the same reason: Bear Bryant.

"I had sorta told the folks at LSU I was coming down there," says Ranager. "But Coach Bryant had asked me not to make up my mind until he had a chance to talk to me. Night before signing day, he came over and met with me.

"He said, 'George, we've got a scholarship for you if you want to come over and play.' I didn't tell anybody, but I made up my mind that night."

Bailey, who remains Alabama's all-time leading receiver, recalls Bryant braving a terrible storm one night to meet with him in Meridian. "I thought, 'Heck, if he wants me bad enough to come out on a night

94

THE BIRMINGHAM NEWS

Archie Manning

like this, the least I can do is play for him,'" Bailey says. "But, really, if you had the opportunity to play for Coach Bryant, you did."

Ranager and Bailey now work together as salesmen for the same hardware company in Meridian. They play golf together at Northwood Country Club. Ranager is a Southeastern Conference football official.

One bit of irony: the receivers coach for Ole Miss in 1969 was Bob Tyler, who coached Ranager and Bailey at Meridian High School.

BOTH teams had visions of winning the SEC championship.

Alabama had lost only four regular-season games the previous five sea-

sons and was off to a 2-0 start with victories over Virginia Tech (17-13) and Southern Mississippi (63-14). Never mind that only three starters returned on defense; the Tide had Bryant, and it had an offense that scored on 10 of 11 possessions against USM.

The Rebels returned 17 starters from a team that finished 6-3-1 the year before. "Ole Miss carries enough ammunition in its football lockers to make a strong run at this year's SEC title, which is what the forecasters have forecast," said the Rebel press guide. A 10-9 loss to Kentucky in the season's second game, following a 28-3 victory over Memphis State, was considered a major fluke.

"During my years at Ole Miss, we

95

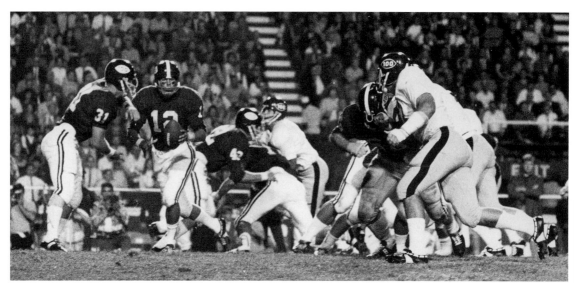

THE BIRMINGHAM NEWS

lost some tough games," Archie says, "but I thought we were always prepared, even when Southern beat us my senior year. Our coaches went out of their way to make sure we weren't complacent.

"But that Kentucky game...I'm not saying we weren't ready to play. I'm just saying our plan that night was like we were saving for Alabama. We ran the Power-I, which is a good formation. But we weren't a Power-I bunch. When you had Floyd Franks and Vernon Studdard and Buddy Jones and Riley Myers, you didn't need one of them in the backfield."

So on the Monday before the Rebels were to play Alabama, Vaught told Archie the game plan. "Let it rip. Bust'em with both barrels. Give'em everything we've got," Archie recalls. "And through the years, Coach Vaught was never really one to do that. But I think he realized that night at Kentucky that he had some explosive people and it was

no sense saving them.

"We had to let Studdard run deep, let Franks work one-on-one, turn Myers loose, get (running back) Leon Felts into the passing game more."

Bryant, sensing the weakness of an Alabama defense that Archie remembers as "not worth a flip," employed the same plan.

Archie's class had never lost to Alabama. In 1967, the Ole Miss freshman won 21-2 in Tuscaloosa. Rebel freshman coach Tom Swayze believed in one-platoon football, and Archie intercepted three passes as a safety that day, despite being knocked silly in the first half.

"I remember the Alabama players walking to the tunnel after the game," says Skip Jernigan, an All-SEC guard at Ole Miss, "and Coach Bryant standing above them in the stands just glaring at them. He was furious."

In 1968, Archie's sophomore season, Ole Miss beat the Tide

96

THE BIRMINGHAM NEWS

LANGSTON ROGERS

Manning and Scott Hunter at the College Football Hall of Fame celebration in New York.

10-8 in Jackson on a field goal by Perry King. Remember that name for future reference.

I T WAS college football's 100th anniversary. Legion Field was decorated with a commemorative emblem, and both teams wore "100" stickers on the side of their helmets.

Dressed in stripeless white jerseys with red numerals, Ole Miss kicked off to Alabama, which was wearing its traditional crimson jerseys with white numerals.

The night's pattern was set early. First play, Hunter passed seven yards to Bailey. "Ole Miss was in a basic (4-4) defense," Bailey recalls. "I'd just find the open area, and Scott was perfect that night."

Replays prove Bailey exactly right. On his first three catches, no fewer than three Ole Miss defenders were surrounding him. Hunter's passes were simply too accurate.

Johnny Musso scored on a 1-yard run, capping a 76-yard, 15-play drive, to make it 7-0 with 8:19 left in the first quarter.

Ole Miss answered that with a 74-yard, 10-play drive to make it 7-7. Archie twice converted third downs into first downs, and the Rebels got a break when Alabama was called for offsides when Ole Miss punted on fourth-and-five at the Tide 39. Manning eventually scored from two yards out.

On a night when the offenses ruled, each defense stood up and took a bow in the second quarter. Nose guard Jeff Horn stopped Alabama fullback Pete Moore on fourth-and-two at the Ole Miss 27. On the ensuing series, Alabama's Danny Gilbert forced Myers to fumble at the Tide four.

Alabama then moved 96 yards in seven plays to take a 14-7 lead. It moved not by Hunter's arm, but instead by an infant formation described by ABC's Wilkinson that night as "the Y." It would later be called the Wishbone. Bryant had been schooled on the advantages of the offense by a gentleman named Emory Bellard, then an assistant coach at Texas.

"It was our going-in and coming-out offense," Ranager says.

On second-and-10 at the Alabama 15, Hunter sprinted right, then pitched almost wildly back to Ranager, who made a splendid one-handed catch. Ole Miss' defense was clearly confused. Ranager was all alone, and only the speed of Rebel safety Glen Cannon, who caught Ranager at the Ole Miss 18, prevented a touchdown.

Ranager suffered a mild ankle sprain on the play. Bubba Sawyer replaced him, and scored two plays later on the same Wishbone play, this time to the left, from 17 yards out. Alabama led 14-7.

Back came Ole Miss. Archie passed 14 yards to Franks, scrambled for 16, then for 17.

Schenkel: "...There's lightning in his every stride."

Archie passed to Studdard for 15, to Franks for 17. The drive ended when Randy Reed was stopped on fourth-and-one at the Alabama 9 with 35 seconds left until halftime.

Hunter fell on the ball twice, taking no chances on blowing the 14-7 lead. In the Alabama dressing room at halftime, Bryant was worried.

"(Bryant) was raising hell and telling us that we had to get off our tails and score some points," says Ranager. "I guess he'd realized by then our defense wasn't worth a (bleep)."

Alabama kicked off to Ole Miss to start the third quarter. "That," says Schenkel, "is when all hell broke loose."

OLE MISS took the second-half kickoff and drove 65 yards in 11 plays to tie the score, converting three third-down plays. Archie passed 11 yards to Franks for the touchdown.

After both teams ran three plays and punted, Alabama pulled ahead 21-14, driving 63 yards in six plays. A 48-yard pass from Hunter to Ranager on the first play moved Alabama to the Ole Miss 15. Musso scored from a yard out.

Three sides later, with 2:30 left in the third quarter, Ole Miss scored again. Felts ran for five, Archie passed 48 yards to tight end Jim Poole down the middle and to Franks for 12 more, then scrambled 17 yards for the touchdown. Alabama 21, Ole Miss 20. Perry King came on for the PAT.

King set a school record for PAT's as a sophomore — 22 of 22 — but for some reason didn't make the trip to Kentucky the week before when Poole's missed PAT proved the difference.

King had made two earlier in the game, but this one slid wide left.

99

"I just missed it," says King, who owns a construction business in Ackerman. "It's something that hangs with you, and you remember it." He says that miss could be what Ole Miss fans remember him for. "But I hope not."

Ole Miss took the lead on its opening possession of the fourth quarter on a two-yard pass from Archie to Myers. The key play of the 86-yard, eight-play march was a 56-yard pass from Archie to Studdard, down to the Alabama 6.

"Coach Vaught had seen Poole wide open down the middle," says Archie, "so he said, 'If Jim can get that open, let's try Studdard.'"

"Vernon came into the huddle and told Jim to go out. I said, 'What in the world are you doing?' He said, 'Coach wants to run tight end streak again.'

"I didn't notice it until the next day on film, but Vernon had no idea how to line up. He got down in a four-point stance and took off."

Franks, who was running an underneath pattern, recalls, "I remember the safety spotting Vernon after he was already in his pattern. I couldn't tell what he was saying, but he was screaming something to the linebacker and he was in a panic."

Ole Miss would try the play again later. "But some big Alabama guy just destroyed Vernon," remembers Tyler.

Archie's two-point conversion pass for Felts was incomplete, but finally Ole Miss had the lead, 26-21.

"It was like there were two Alabama teams out there," says Bailey.

"At one end of the bench were the offensive coaches, who had everything running smooth. And on the other end of the bench, where the defensive coaches were, it was pandemonium. They were screaming and yelling. It was kind of amusing to watch it all."

Alabama regained the lead with a 67-yard, 10-play drive, capped by Hunter's one-yard TD sneak. The try for two was no good. Alabama 27, Ole Miss 26 with 7:43 left.

Twenty-eight seconds later, Ole Miss led 32-27. Manning passed 42 yards to Studdard, scrambled for 21, then sneaked a yard for the score. Again the two-point try failed.

With 7:15 to play, Alabama set out on its 80-yard, game-winning drive. A pass to Bailey for nine. Pete Jilleba ran for 16. A pass to Steve Doran for 15, another pass to Bailey for 13. Hunter was sacked by Dennis Coleman for minus-eight yards, but Hunter came back with an 18-yard strike to Bailey.

That set up first-and-10 at the Ole Miss 14. Less than five minutes remained.

On first down, Ranager was stopped for no gain on the same Wishbone pitchout that had worked so well in the first half. Two passes were incomplete. Alabama faced fourth-and-10 at the 14. Less than four minutes remained when Alabama called timeout. Ranager and Hunter went to the sideline to confer with Bryant.

"Get me the ball," Ranager said.

"What do you want to run?" Hunter asked Bryant, who posed the same question to offensive coach

Jimmy Sharpe.

N.M. Cavette, the linesman, warned the Tide coaches that the time-out was almost over.

"Get me the ball," Ranager insisted again.

"OK," said Bryant. "Run Pro Right, 56X Circle. That's your best pass play."

As Hunter went back to pass, Rebel defensive end Johnny Gilliland came in untouched. Hunter never acknowledged the pressure and fired a strike toward Ranager.

Fred Farmer, "the fastest sideback in the Reb secondary," according to the Ole Miss press guide, was guarding Ranager. As Ranager made an inside move, the two collided. Farmer fell to the ground and was called for pass interference. Somehow, Ranager stayed on his feet. He looked up just as the ball arrived.

Schenkel: "...Look at this!"

Ranager caught the ball at the four, then leaped into the end zone. The first Alabama player to greet Ranager was center Richard Grammer, who would die in a hunting accident three days after the season finale.

Alabama 33, Ole Miss 32 with 3:42 to play. Once again, the try for two failed.

The Rebels didn't fold. A nine-yard pass to Poole produced a fourth-and-one situation at the Alabama 49. Archie sneaked, but was stopped cold.

Alabama took over with 2:24 left, ran three plays, then punted to the Ole Miss five where the ball was downed by Ranager.

Ninety-five yards away, 1:48 left.

One point behind.

Archie missed on two passes. "Without sounding too dramatic," says Franks, "with each incompletion, it was like watching a little more of your life chopped off."

Archie scrambled in the end zone and got off a third-down completion to Felts that netted minus-two yards. But he regained the magic on fourth-and-12 at the Rebel three to pass 15 yards to Myers, who made a nifty move at the 12 to secure the first down.

Ole Miss got a break two plays later when Alabama was called for a facemask violation. First-and-10 at the Rebel 34 with 15 seconds left.

Wilkinson: "...One long pass and a field goal from winning."

Whenever in trouble, Archie always seemed to look for Franks, a studious receiver who survived on brains as much as athletic ability. He caught 13 passes that night, an SEC record at the time. His 12th catch went for 17 yards to the Alabama 49 with eight seconds left.

Archie again threw to Franks, who caught the ball at the 42. "I was trying to get to the sideline," Franks recalls, "but an Alabama guy tripped me up before I could get out of bounds.

"I looked up at the referee and called timeout, and he looked me square in the eye and did nothing. I watched the clock and with each second that ticked off I kept getting this...I don't know...a feeling that all was lost. I know you shouldn't get those feelings about a football game, but we had been in combat for hours. It was quite a rollercoaster ride."

Coach John Vaught being introduced to the ABC-TV audience by Bill Fleming.

Franks thought that the referee was crooked. Not until years later did he finally learn that Ole Miss had used all its timeouts.

Schenkel (sounding like his dog had just died): "...Time has run out on the Rebels of Mississippi."

After the game, the Ole Miss players were in shock. Never before had a Rebel team scored 32 points and lost. A pre-season favorite to win the SEC title, they were now 0-2 in the league.

"We simply couldn't believe we had lost," says Skip Jernigan. "I mean, we had marched up and down the field. It just seemed we were so much better than they were. It was a mystery."

Vaught called it "the most emotional game I've ever been involved in."

The TV cameras showed Archie in tears as he walked off the field. He cried only twice more during his college career — before and after the 1970 Mississippi State game, when the Bulldogs won 19-14 with Archie sidelined with a broken arm.

Rebel defensive back Ray Heidel was crying too. His ear lobe had been nearly torn off while making a tackle in the first quarter. It was held together the final three periods by a Band-Aid. Doctors sewed it back on post-game without the use of a pain killer.

"I remember sitting there in the dressing room talking to (fullback) Bo Bowen," says Archie. "We were about as down as we'd ever been. Then someone showed us the stats. That only made it worse."

102

Ole Miss defeated Georgia the next week 25-17, won eight of 11 games and finished eighth in the nation after beating Arkansas 27-22 in the Sugar Bowl.

Alabama lost the next week to Vanderbilt 14-10 and finished 6-5, its worst record since 1958, Bear Bryant's first year there.

Archie went on to become an All-America quarterback, a 1970 Heisman Trophy candidate, the National Football Conference's 1978 Player of the Year and MVP.

But no matter how many years pass or how many awards he receives, Archie can't forget the special feeling he had that night in Birmingham.

"When I talk to kids, I talk to them about making football fun," he says. "And that's the most fun I ever had. For a quarterback, what could be more fun than throwing the ball almost every down, completing them and scoring? That's what it's all about."

The Dog Comes Home

By Willie Morris

The Dog Comes Home

To OUR TORTURED and beautiful locale, as my friends are saying: "The Dog's come home." And indeed he has—Billy (Dog) Brewer. He has inherited the once-mighty Ole Miss Rebels football team, a decade of losing, in a university that rightly or wrongly has a dubious national reputation on race. Just as I did after many years of American wanderings, he has returned at last to his native Mississippi.

It will not be easy for Dog, who is the first to admit it. He succeeds Steve Sloan, who left for Duke after Ole Miss did not win a game in the Southeastern Conference, and the predictions for 1983 have the Rebels near the bottom of this most tempestuous league.

"I want to rebuild Ole Miss and make it a winner again," Dog says to me. He was a physical player as a quarterback and defensive back for Ole Miss in the late 1950s, baptized in the blood of Johnny Vaught football. He never took over a team that was a winner, and he never left one a loser. At Lee High and later at Heritage Academy in Columbus, Miss., he turned losers into winners, and he did the same at Southeastern Louisiana and Louisiana Tech. Tech was 3-8 when he took over as head coach, and three years later, in 1982, was 10-3 and reached the semifinals of the Division I-AA playoffs.

He is a rigorous disciplinarian who does not like to lose. He is also a gambler against the elements. Against highly favored Texas A&M in College Station last year, his Louisiana Tech team passed 62 times and almost upset the Aggies. He once called for an onside kick on an opening kickoff. "In the last five years," Pat Dye, the Auburn coach, said last week, "Ole Miss hasn't hit a lick at a snake. But Brewer's team will scratch and claw you to death."

Willie Morris

He was a physical player as a quarterback and defensive back for Ole Miss in the late 1950s, baptized in the blood of Johnny Vaught football. He never took over a team that was a winner, and he never left one a loser. He is a rigorous disciplinarian who does not like to lose. He is also a gambler . . . He once called for an onside kick on the opening kickoff.

This article by Willie Morris appeared prominently in The New York Times on Sunday, August 28, 1983, one week before the start of Billy Brewer's first football season at Ole Miss. It was subsequently reprinted in a number of America's largest newspapers. There was a touch of prophecy in this article.

COMMERCIAL DISPATCH

In 1983 Chancellor Porter Fortune and Athletic Director Warner Alford ushered in a new era in Rebel football: new Head Coach Billy Brewer had arrived.

I FIRST met Dog when he came back to Oxford last Christmas, just in time for the annual bachelors' party at Shine Morgan's Furniture Store on the square. We are the same age, of the same Mississippi generation, and we share many of the same friends. We became comrades, I believe, because of our love of animals and sports, and because we are amused and saddened by many of the same things. My dog Pete, a Black Labrador who was the brother of my middle years, had just died. Dog wanted to visit his grave to pay his deferences. I was just finishing a book on Marcus Dupree. Dog was interested in that, too.

He has pale blue eyes, sandy hair, and he likes a dip of snuff. I under-stood what his friend, a businessman in Memphis named Larry McKnight, had told me of him: "He has the intensity of a world-class chess player and the heart of a lion. He'll stick with you. That's Dog Brewer." Some college football coaches might pass for the new bank president who is in charge of the keys to the vault in a middle-sized city on the rise. Others remind me of Jaycee program chairmen, Jerry Falwell evangelists, computer technocrats, and condominium developers. Many have faces upon which the accumulated fratricides of college football seem to have settled. Dog is as Mississippi as the Tallahatchie River; I am happy, too, to detect a sly Dixie humor and an absence of paranoia. And he exudes

an ineffable drama, which will hold him in good stead in the days ahead.

Dog loves dogs. He owns several Black Labs and various other hybrid species who have journeyed with him from Louisiana. When he was 11 years old in Columbus he had a dog named Peewee. One day he and McKnight and two black friends named Slick and Bubba saw Peewee run over and killed. The driver of the car kept going. Sobbing insanely, Dog picked up some rocks and ran after the car as it sped away. Later, at the burial, Dog remembers Slick's eulogy:

Ashes to ashes,
Dust to dust
Poor Ol' Peewee
Done hushed his fuss.

There are some 700 black students at Ole Miss, roughly seven percent of the enrollment. Black students have complained that they do not feel they are a significant part of campus life, and that the traditional symbols of the Old South—the fight song "Dixie," the mascot Colonel Rebel, and the waving of the Confederate flag at games are insulting. The university has withdrawn its sanction of the Confederate flag, and a rendition of "Dixie" and "The Battle Hymn of the Republic" played by the Ole Miss band at games would touch the soul of a Massachusetts abolitionist. Yet the complaints persist. The football team is half white and half black and the black players are genuine campus heroes.

The competition for high school football players in Mississippi between

Ole Miss, Mississippi State and Southern Mississippi had become suicidal. It is an underpopulated state with three major football powers. The challenge for Ole Miss football has had much to do with recruiting the outstanding black players.

Although he feels, as do I, that Mississippi may have come further than any other state racially, Dog Brewer admits such a national image of Ole Miss exists, aided by the rumors circulated by rival recruiters. "One way to solve it is to win. With the positive attitude our team has now—the oneness and love this team has, black and white—we can overcome any obstacles."

He arrives with a reputation for recruiting blacks and for getting along well with them, a father figure of sorts. On the wall of his office is a large silver plaque given him by Horace Wayne Belton, the distinguished black running back in Dog's days at Southeastern Louisiana: "To Coach Brewer. Thanks for three super years."

Horace Wayne Belton would often come to dinner at Dog and Kay's (the lovely Mrs. Dog). On one such visit Dog had just bought a most handsome Black Labrador puppy.

"Horace Wayne," Dog asked, "what do you think of my new puppy?"

"He's black," Horace Wayne replied, "and black sure is beautiful. What's his name, Coach?"

"His name is Horace Wayne Belton."

Clyde Goolsby, the black bar-

tender at my favorite saloon in Oxford and a most powerful man in town because, like Nick Carraway in "The Great Gatsby", he is privy to the secret grief of wild, unknown men, knows Dog and helps him advise the black athletes: "I've looked Dog over close. He's a good man within himself. The black athletes love him. They say, 'I wish I'd had Dog Brewer before now. Dog don't pick color.' These kids will appreciate him even more after the journey is over."

Dog himself predicts he will do well recruiting the black athletes. He mentions Ben Williams, the first Ole Miss black player, now with the Buffalo Bills, who helps him recruit. "I understand the Southern black. I grew up with them. I lived on Fourteenth Avenue in Columbus, Miss., down the end of the street and over the railroad. That's where I met 'T' Thomas, our new assistant. We played football every Sunday afternoon on a sawdust pile. I was the only white boy allowed to play. It was the place to be."

The halcyon days of Ole Miss football are still obsessively remembered here—the unbeaten seasons, the bowl games, the All-Americans, the national rankings. Only Ole Miss football seemed to hold the university and the state together when Mississippi was down and out. "It must've been something here in the 1950s and 60s," a student now says. "Faulkner won the Nobel Prize, and then there were the Miss Americas, and all the Ole Miss Rhodes Scholars, and the Rebels winning." And an older home expert adds: "I've seen this football team save the university from adversity before. It's on the brink of doing it again."

111

Quarterback/defensive back (1958-60).

Brewer with friend Willie Morris.

LANGSTON ROGERS

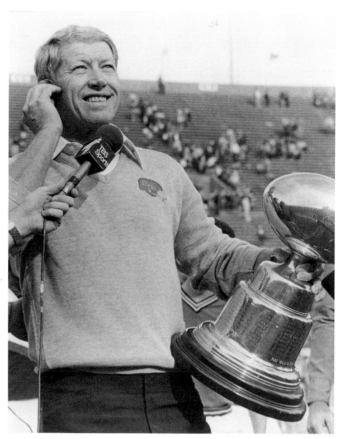

With 1984 Egg Bowl trophy.

With linebacker Tony "Gator" Bennett.

MARK HALL

112

Scoring a touchdown in the Red and Blue "Old-Timers" game.

MARK HALL

With Auburn Coach Pat Dye

113

The 1983 Ole Miss football staff: (front row, l-r) David Hines, Robert McGraw, Billy Brewer, Carl Torbush, Ron Case, (back row, l-r) Blake Barnes, Bill Canty, Robert Youngblood, James T. Thomas, George Smith, Mickey Merritt, and Leroy Mullins.

IT WILL not be a perfunctory rebuilding. The 1983 team, Dog says, which has one of the nation's most difficult schedules, is "thin as tissue paper on depth. What we found here wasn't a great deal of talent, but there's nothing we can do about that now. We'll try to win with it. We've concentrated on work habits and attitude. For the first time in a long while they have confidence in themselves. I want my players to feel the closeness we had back then. Winning when I played here was a tradition. We'll get it back. Every day I wake up I say, 'I'm back home at Ole Miss.'"

Gentleman though he was, Steve Sloan was a Tennessean who never really understood this bewitched and complicated state, and in the end it may have defeated him. Dog Brewer knows and loves it—its white and black people—and comprehends its rare promise. Mississippi is at the crossroads now. Its capstone state university, by the nature of universities, must lead. This lovely old campus with its history of suffering and adversity is ready for him. He is a repository of hope here for more than football itself.

In the Spirit of the Game

By Willie Morris

In the Spirit of the Game

THIS IS a tale not of one Game Day but two, because each was deeply enmeshed in the other.

It begins with the Ole Miss-Vanderbilt game of October 28, 1989, in Oxford, Mississippi. It was Ole Miss Homecoming, one of those Southern autumn days touched with the airy bittersweet langour of the past and memory and childhood...and football.

Ole Miss is small by measure with other state universities, with 10,000 students—roughly the same population as the town—who are suffused with the flamboyant elan of their contemporaries everywhere. In moments there is a palpable, affecting sophistication to its stunningly beautiful campus in the rolling rural woodlands of the South. On this Homecoming day, one might recall Thomas Wolfe's only slightly fictional Pulpit Hill, patterned after the Chapel Hill of many years ago in Look Homeward, Angel: "There was still a good flavor of the wilderness about the place—one felt its remoteness, its isolated charm. It seemed to Eugene like a provincial outpost of great Rome: The wilderness crept up to it like a beast."

Two hours before the kickoff, the young men of the Ole Miss team, led by Coach Billy "Dog" Brewer, walked single file through the Grove, a huge old verdant circle only a stone's throw from the stadium, as avid tailgaters applauded. From the distance the band played "From Dixie With Love," a blended rendition of "Dixie" and "The Battle Hymn of the Republic." As the mighty sounds wafted across this wooded terrain, little girls in the school's Harvard red and Yale blue tossed and leapt, and miniature quarterbacks in replica jerseys threw footballs to incipient Rebel wide receivers. The adults were drinking, and everywhere was the ineffable cachet of fried chicken and barbecue. On one lengthy table draped with a vintage Delta tablecloth were eight-branch silver candelabra with red taper candles and mounds of food on matching silver trays. On another was a substantial arrangement of flowers flowing out of an Ole Miss football helmet—lacy white fragile baby's-breath and red carnations.

The stadium itself, surrounded by its young magnolias,

ALEN MACWEENEY

Willie Morris

"I couldn't get off the sideline. In all the years I've been coaching, it's the first time I haven't gone on the field when there was a serious injury. I couldn't go. I thought the kid was dead. No matter how long I coach, I'll always remember how he came flying through the air and made the hit."
—Billy Brewer

Chucky Mullins,
defensive back

the dense history of a school that has often played out the richest and darkest passions of the region."

There is a special flavor, a texture, to Deep Southern collegiate football, and this was best expressed years ago by Marino Casem, the long-time coach at Alcorn University:

> In the East college football is a cultural exercise.
> On the West coast it is a tourist attraction.
> In the Midwest it is cannibalism.
> But in the Deep South it is religion, and Saturday is the holy day.

THERE WAS indeed a religiosity to this crowd in the moments before game time. In the south end zone a loyalist group perennially regarded as The Rowdies, a perfervid cadre consisting of professors, bartenders, writers, and reprobates, shouted epithets at the visitors down from their cerebral Nashville halls: "Down with the Eggheads! Stomp the Existentialists!" A Yankee reporter, surveying this end zone phalanx, asked one of its number, Dean Faulkner Wells, niece of the home-town bard, why she supported Ole Miss football. With a succinctness uncharacteristic of the Faulkner breed, she replied: "Continuity."

The record of the Ole Miss team at this juncture was five wins, two losses. It was hobbled with injuries. At one point the entire starting defensive backfield was down, including football and academic All-America safety Todd Sandroni, who

was cozy and contained, and much removed from the mega-stadiums of the SEC behemoths Alabama and Auburn and Tennessee and Georgia and LSU and Florida. Its grassy turf had seen Bruiser Kinard, Charlie Conerly, Barney Poole, Jake Gibbs, Squirrel Griffin, Gene Hickerson, Archie Manning, and Gentle Ben Williams. There were 34,500 in attendance on this afternoon, including a smattering of Vandy partisans down from Tennessee in their bright-gold colors matching the golden patina of this day. At Ole Miss, The New York Times would report of what was to follow, "The game blends into

118

PAT MANER

Chucky Mullins and Coach Billy Brewer

was playing on one good leg. The Rebels' largest margin of victory had been seven points. They had upset Florida on the road by four while gaining only 128 offensive yards. They had defeated Georgia on a touchdown pass with 31 seconds to go in this stadium, and Tulane on another pass in New Orleans with four seconds remaining. It was a funny, gritty ball club, small and hurt in the mighty SEC, a ball club people could not help but love.

There was 6:57 left in the first quarter when it happened.

Vandy faced third and goal from the Ole Miss 12 in a scoreless game. Quarterback John Gromos faded for the pass. Brad Gaines, the 210-pound fullback, caught it on the two. Roy Lee "Chucky" Mullins, the 175-pound Ole Miss cornerback,

suddenly raced across the field, leapt high, and tackled the receiver, forcing him to drop the football. The resounding thud could be heard for yards around. Cheers rolled across the stadium. But Mullins lay prone on the field, and when he did not move, a fateful quiet descended.

"I couldn't get off the sideline," Ole Miss coach Dog Brewer would later recall. "In all the years I've been coaching, it's the first time I haven't gone on the field when there was a serious injury. I couldn't go. I thought the kid was dead. No matter how long I coach, I'll always remember how he came flying through the air and made the hit—the thud of it."

The silent throng watched as the trainers and doctor cut Mullins' face mask away and strapped him to a wooden board. It took them more than 10 horrible minutes. Then they carried him to the opposite sidelines, and the ambulance slowly wound its way out of the stadium toward the hospital. The scene would not easily be obliterated.

The rest of the first half seemed bitter anticlimax. The flat, listless Ole Miss team fell behind 10-0. Chucky Mullins' injury likewise cast an ominous pall over the Homecoming rituals of halftime, the Ole Miss beauties in evening dresses, the playing of the alma mater.

How to explain such human moments? Ole Miss came out in the third quarter on fire, then erupted in the fourth. Trailing 17-16, Ole Miss took over on its own 21 with 9:18 remaining. Halfback Tyrone Ashley carried twice for 13 yards, then quar-

120

terback John Darnell hit tight end Rich Gebbia of Long Island ("our own Yankee") for 49 yards to the Commodore 17. On the ensuing play Ashley broke free for the winning touchdown with 7:18 left. The game ended 24-17.

In the locker room the Ole Miss players were choked up over their fallen teammate. There was no celebration after this one.

Sometime in the second half Chucky had been flown to Memphis, 75 miles away. The small hospital in Oxford could do little but stabilize his condition. He lay now in neurosurgery intensive care in the Baptist Memorial Hospital.

He was paralyzed from the neck down. The injury was serious, with little likelihood that he would ever recover. The attending doctors would call it one of the most drastic injuries they had ever seen, likening the impact that crushed his back to the crushing of an empty can. The vertebrae had exploded; there was nothing left. On the Monday after homecoming four surgeons performed a three-hour operation using wire and bone graft from Chucky's pelvis to fuse the shattered vertebrae. He would remain a quadriplegic.

The mood of the university, the town, and the state in the following days was of grief and sadness. Ole Miss dedicated the rest of the season to him.

In 1987 Chucky Mullins, a 17-year-old from the tiny town of Russellville, in northwest Alabama, came to Ole Miss, one of many poor young blacks signed each year by the

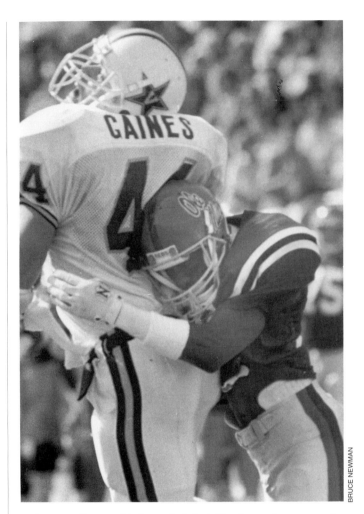

When Mullins tackled Vanderbilt fullback Brad Gaines, the impact shattered his vertebrae.

Rebels. When he was recruited and given an athletic scholarship, he did not have the money to get to Oxford. His mother had died, so he was raised by a legal guardian, Carver Phillips, who suffered from a debilitating lung disease. In his senior year in high school, Chucky was the football captain. Both Auburn and Alabama considered him too small and slow, and he wanted to go to Ole Miss.

He was Dog Brewer's kind of

Chucky Mullins at the Liberty Bowl with (l-r): Karen Phillips, Warner Alford, Dick Hackett, Chancellor Gerald Turner and Carver Phillips, Chucky's legal guardian.

athlete: "He was lanky, always clapping, having fun, what we call a 'glue' player, not that fast or big, but the kind that holds a team together. What you saw him wearing was damn near what he owned. But to see him, you'd think he was a millionaire."

Chucky's best friend on the Ole Miss team was a white freshman named Trea Southerland. After the operation in Memphis two days after the Vandy game, Chucky came out of the anesthesia whispering Southerland's name. "Chucky added a lot to other people's lives," Southerland said. "And I know that if desire and character make a differ-

ence, he'll find a way to beat this."

A chance photograph before the Vanderbilt Homecoming game had caught a pristine moment. Coach Brewer and Mullins are standing together in the north end zone, not far from where Chucky would soon be hurt, the coach's arm around number 38's waist as the two of them led the team onto the field. It was a gesture of symbolic affinity: Brewer was also from a poor family and a broken home, attending Ole Miss in its glory days as a "step slow" ball player. "When you love the game, it has a hold on you," Brewer says of Mullins, but it is an autobio-

Chucky Mullins and Carver Phillips greeted by Archie Manning.

graphical confession too. "I kind of saw myself in him. The only way out for both of us was football."

Ole Miss was matched the next Saturday against the Bayou Bengals of LSU. For the first time since 1960, this tumultuous and historic rivalry would be played in Oxford.

Within hours of Chucky Mullins' injury a trust fund had been started for him. LSU collected donations at its Purple-Gold basketball game in Baton Rouge. The University of Delaware shut down a football practice an hour early for a prayer session. Calls from coaches—and the White House—came in from all over America. Coach Bill Curry, then of Alabama, collected donations from his players. "Statistics tell us,"

Chucky and defensive back Chris "Creek" Mitchell, who wore Chucky's #38 jersey in 1990, emblem of the Chucky Mullins Courage Award.

BILL ROGERS

In 1992 Billy Brewer and film star Alan Autry awarded the "Chucky Mullins Courage" jersey to Trea Southerland.

Curry said, "that football is a very safe game when you're talking about catastrophic injuries. Ankles? Knees? Fingers? No, it's not safe. But not one time in a billion do you see the kind of injury that happened to Chucky Mullins."

Mike Archer, the LSU coach, visited Chucky in the hospital Friday night before the Saturday game. "I can understand how this has affected their team," he said. "I almost broke down with tears when I visited with him. It hurts to see a strong, healthy kid like that, so young."

Shortly before the game, seven Ole Miss men in the finals for "Colonel Reb," the campus's highest accolade, withdrew from the election and swung the honor to Mullins.

The LSU match would be one of the most dramatic moments in Ole

Miss sports annals. The Rebel players wore number 38 on their helmets. The largest crowd in the history of the little stadium, 42,354, turned out for the contest. Hundreds of Ole Miss students volunteered to pass buckets during the game for the trust fund. More than $240,000 would be collected at this game alone, five times more than the goal.

Chucky Mullins was listening on the radio in the intensive care unit in Memphis. Just prior to the kickoff there was a prayer for his welfare.

The win over Vandy the previous Saturday had given 6-2 Ole Miss an opportunity at the SEC title and a chance at its first Sugar Bowl since 1970. Yet devastation struck the Rebels early, and it was obvious that they were taut with emotion—fumbles, incomplete passes, penalties. LSU quarterback Tom Hodson was magnificent, and the Tigers jumped to a swift 21-0 lead. The score was 35-10 late in the third period, and the LSU depth was showing.

Then, suddenly, as they had all year against adversity, the Rebels, outweighed and outmanned at nearly every position, crippled by injury and despair, came alive in the final quarter. Quarterback Darnell's formerly errant passes began to click, and slashing runs by sophomores Randy Baldwin and Tyrone Ashley left gaping holes in the Louisiana phalanx. The Rebel players were yelling to each other after each big play: "This one's for Chucky! We're gonna do it!"

The score was now LSU 35, Ole Miss 30. The Rebels were driving from their own territory as the game ebbed away. A burnt orange sun was descending behind Vaught-Hemingway Stadium, and the air was eerie with the early dark. The entire assemblage was on its feet, and the partisan fans were stomping in unison, filling the hazy mystic afternoon with the pandemonium of fealty.

Twenty-five seconds remained now, and the Rebels had first and 10 on the LSU 30. Quarterback Darnell, injured five plays before, limped back onto the field. An uncommon hush descended, and a member of the south end zone Rowdies fell out of a lower row of the bleachers.

As the play unfolded, Darnell hobbled back into the pocket. The nimble wide receiver, Willie Green, streaked toward the south end zone,

covered only by cornerback Jimmy Young, four inches shorter. It only took seconds. The ball was in flight now, suspended it seemed for the briefest eternity etched against the waning horizon, as Willie Green leapt high, arms outraised in one quick pirouette of hope.

The pass came up two feet short. The Bayou Bengals defender, high in the air with Green, intercepted in the end zone, then fell lovingly to the turf, ball in breast.

If the Rebels had scored, they would have led 36-35 with 20 seconds left. Going for and making the two-point conversion, they would have achieved a symbolic 38.

Yet life often does not work that way. A great sporting event indeed emulates life, its ecstasies and sorrows, its gallantries and failures, and its time running out, the time that runs out in Dixie autumn twilights for all of us who wish life to give us feeling and victory and hope against old mortality. The Bayou Bengals intercepted, 20 seconds left. Only the love remained, and the possibility.

125

In the End Zone

By Larry Wells

In the End Zone

EVERYTHING LOOKS different from the end zone. Depth perception is tricky. Five-yard gains are actually ten. Plays seem to break faster. It's hard to see who has the ball. The quarterback rolls out to pass but suddenly a ballcarrier comes skittering through the line of scrimmage, loose and dangerous. Endzoners share the panic of linebackers reacting late, or the joy of a tight end open over the middle. During field goal attempts, we're the first fans in the stadium to know whether the kick is good or bad and alertly signal the results before the referees. As if the game is being recorded in stereo we observe first the home fans rising to cheer on one side of the stadium, then the visitors slumping in misery on the other. Such a perspective sometimes gives endzoners a strange objectivity, a feeling of being above it all, except when opposing fans are ringing cowbells in our faces. When the action is at the far end of the field, distance acts as a kind of buffer, but when the visitors mount a drive toward our end zone we become intimately involved.

Eleven offensive plays from inside the ten coming right at us.

The end zone can be both heaven and hell. If one doesn't feel anything, he is either a humanoid or a saint—and in the south end zone of Vaught-Hemingway Stadium there are neither.

As with so many of life's happy decisions we came to the south end zone by chance. Throughout the 1970s, my wife Dean and I bought tickets to the Ole Miss home games as well as those in Memphis. Dean had attended Ole Miss as an undergraduate and had been a Rebel fan practically from birth. Her father, Dean Swift Faulkner, had lettered in baseball at the University in the 1930s and had briefly been a "scrub" on the football team. [Note: See related article on p. 21] I, on the other hand, had attended the University of Alabama and had been a Tide fan exclusively until 1970 when I entered Ole Miss and enlisted in Archie's Army.

In those days we sat on the student side of Vaught-Hemingway Stadium. They weren't great seats but we were

Larry Wells

Of all the things that matter, birth and death and forgiveness and humility and hope and love, what else could have made us weep and laugh and grasp the hands of strangers in red and blue? We were one tribe, one nation, indivisible, with victory and glad tidings for all.

happy to be there. After all, our team was winning. I assumed, in those heady days, that Ole Miss would always be a contender for the conference title. I had seen ABC-TV's 1969 "shootout" between Archie Manning and Scott Hunter and knew about Billy Cannon's legendary punt return a decade earlier. I enjoyed, but took for granted, the aerial magic of Manning-to-Franks, marveled at, yet fully expected, Vaught's patented offense to keep on rolling. I had no idea what was waiting in the future—the tough years, the "hang on and pray" seasons when we grew lean with defeat, joked about building character and prayed for Warner Alford to find a coach who could do the impossible: rebuild while recruiting against two other Division I-A universities in a sparsely populated state and competing in the toughest college league in America.

Looking down at the wooden bleachers in the south end zone (the only end zone seating in those days—the north end zone stands not being constructed until 1979), one could not help noticing that it seated primarily African-American fans. I wondered how the stadium looked to the endzoners in those days—white fans cheering for white boys—wondered, also, how they felt a year or two later when Ben Williams led the Rebels onto the field. I believe the first high-fives in Vaught-Hemingway occurred in the south end zone when Williams jumped offsides on the first play of

the game and sacked both the center and the quarterback. Yet long before Williams had broken the color barrier, Ole Miss football enjoyed the support of many black fans. I admired those good citizens of the south end zone, who must have known that time was on their side.

In 1970 Southern Mississippi gave Ole Miss a wakeup call behind the running of a lightning-quick back with an unexpectedly Nordic name. Willie Heidelburg's praises were sung (grudgingly) by many Rebel students as we left the stadium. The end of an era had arrived and we had begun to feel the effects of the transition. Maybe it was time for us to sit in the end zone. Maybe that was where we had belonged, all along.

Over the years Dean has played tennis with the coach's wives. Women's tennis is superior to men's in that it's not just for exercise. Secrets are shared, spiritual support given and received. Dean always knew which coach got the most credit for a win or what key players were injured or who was going to be red-shirted. Balls were hit more crisply, however, if the Rebels had lost. If Dean got hit in the head she didn't complain. In that close circle, tears were never shed. There is nobody tougher on earth than coaches' wives. Dean played with Shirley Crawford, Noonie Carmody (both during the Kinard-Cooper eras and more recently in the Brewer), Kay Cooper and Brenda Sloan—not to mention Nancy

Weltlich. We soon were enmeshed more deeply than ever in Ole Miss football, screaming ourselves hoarse on Saturday and enduring morgue-like Sundays when cars drove to church like hearses.

It was during the Sloan era that we became south end zone regulars. Willie Morris had recently moved to Oxford and had begun his brilliant tenure as the University's journal-ist-in-residence. Ole Miss football had been one of the attractions with which we lured him back from New York. We saw every home game in 1980 together, usually sitting in the west stands about halfway up, on the twenty-five yard line. Those Rebel teams had a habit of building an early lead, then sitting on it—abandoning an aggressive offense and playing conservatively. The audience would grow silent, chilled by foreboding as the sun burned their backs. The Rebels usually ran a dive or counter play and then on third down (Willie leaping up and yelling, "Throw the _____ ball!") an option or a draw, often into the teeth of the defense. Never one to disguise his feelings, Morris occa-sionally offended nearby fans who objected not to his playcalling but presumably to his choice of phrase.

In 1983, Billy Brewer's home-coming season as head coach, enthusiasm abounded and tickets were harder to come by. We found ourselves, one hot afternoon, sitting in the south end zone. It was there that we witnessed the birth of an era, as the Rebels started slow but finished strong and went on to play

Professor David Sansing, "Emperor" of the south end zone, with "Associate Athletic Director" Willie Morris.

Writers Dean Faulkner Wells and Barry Hannah belt out the national anthem.

131

WALT MIXON

Quarterback Russ Shows (14) showed poise and made few errors.

WALT MIXON

Cory Philpot (30) scores against State on a quick opener.

in the Independence Bowl. When Red Parker took over as offensive coordinator, Morris was seen making the sign of the cross and blessing "Good Red Parker, good Red Parker."

At first, our group was small: Willie and Dean and me, occasionally joined by our sons, David Morris and Jon Mallard. Then David Sansing and Ron Borne of the Ole Miss faculty joined us, along with their wives, Lib

and Jane. At the Georgia game, Morris was interviewed on both the Bulldog and Rebel radio networks, and the south end zone began to come into its own. In the early eighties Barry Hannah moved to Oxford to teach at the University. He and his wife Susan soon became fixtures in the end zone. Longtime Rebel fans Ron Shapiro, Jane Rule Burdine, Richard Howorth, Elizabeth Dollarhide and Jim Dees joined us. The press took notice, calling us the South Endzone Rowdies (or Bleacher Bums, depending on whom they interviewed). Susan Hannah even made a banner which was displayed on the front of the stands. We had a mutant Visiting Writers Lectureship program, featuring such notables as Raad Cawthen and John Little, who delivered opinions (or toasts) at half-time. On any given Saturday our number was swelled by movie producers, actors, magazine editors, literary agents and former Rebel football stars. A writers and artists colony had sprung up in the south end zone. "Where else could this have happened," Morris would ask, "except in a stadium named Hemingway?"

One Saturday afternoon in 1991, we invited the photographer Bill Eggleston, an Ole Miss alumnus, to sit with us. Not a football fan by choice, he nevertheless was interested in seeing a game. I don't think he had attended a game before, or if he had, he didn't remember it. He watched politely, though his attention wandered. I turned to him, exclaiming over a quarterback sack, and found him staring at a hot air balloon drifting past the stadium, perhaps willing it to fly back against the wind. Suddenly everyone erupted into applause and Eggleston glanced at us in surprise as if wondering why anyone cared about young men in shoulder pads and helmets running into each other. Still, he enjoyed the color and excitement, the pageantry and drama.

We held south end zone pep rallies at the Hoka Theatre across from the Gin Company in Oxford. Sansing was elected president by acclamation. His first (and only to date) official act was to announce a change in title, from President to Emperor. Endzoners brought good luck charms and "mojos" which were passed around for later use and quoted fiery speeches from Knute Rockne or Bear Bryant or William Faulkner. The night before the 1992 Ole Miss-State game, the first time the arch rivals had played in Oxford in twenty years, we needed some industrial strength inspiration. Dean suggested her favorite passage from Faulkner's The Bear. Ron Shapiro, Jim Dees and Semmes Luckett later held a midnight ceremony on the fifty yard line at Vaught-Hemingway, took off their hats and by the flame of a cigarette lighter invoked Mr. Bill's blessing:

Who else could have made them fight: could have struck them so aghast with fear and dread as to turn shoulder to shoulder and face one way and even stop talking for a while and even after

Cassius "B." Ware (40) with a quarterback sack as Dewayne Dotson (33) closes in.

Artis Ford (70) pressures State quarterback Greg Plump.

two years of it keep them still so wrung with terror that some among them would seriously propose moving their very capital into a foreign country lest it be ravaged and pillaged...Who else could have declared a war against a power with ten times the area and a hundred times the men and a thousand times the resources, except men who could believe that all necessary to conduct a successful war was not acumen nor shrewdness nor politics nor diplomacy nor money nor even integrity and simple arithmetic but just love of land and courage.

"And the ability to kick a field goal," Dean added later, "don't leave that out!"

The day of the State game dawned grey and chill. Fortified by determination and other spirits, Bums and Rowdies took their seats behind the goalposts, surrounded by Bulldogs (the end zone being sold out mostly to State fans). The aluminum benches were like ice; blankets and cushions were absolute necessities. Our mojos included a Haitian cross made by Jim Weems of wood and feathers, various antique brooches and plastic buttons, seashells (don't ask why), and Jane Rule's battered French horn (to drown out any cowbells). Ole Miss was a one-point favorite, which was meaningless since our injury-plagued offensive line had been rebuilt from scratch in two weeks. Quarterback Russ Shows would be under immense pressure to execute and not make mistakes. We hovered between hope and terror though we never let the Bulldog fans know it. Shapiro and Howorth vied to tell the best State joke, including one or two about veterinary medicine.

The game began. As if through a single pair of eyes, we watched the score seesaw back and forth. At halftime State held a 10-7 advantage. Then the Rebels came from behind in the third quarter and were leading by a touchdown in the fourth.

Now came a rare sequence of events which Hannah called "the ultimate test of manhood"—eleven plays from inside the Rebel ten yardline, not to be imagined in our wildest nightmares, and in *our* end zone! Somehow the Rebels held. Defensive tackle Chad Brown saw the opposing guard pulling and shot through to tackle the ballcarrier for a loss. Frosh safety Michael Lowery intercepted a pass by State quarterback Todd Jordan. On the next play, however, the Rebels fumbled it back. Susan Hannah was holding up the Haitian mojo with her eyes closed, repeating a mantra: "Stay out of our end zone, stay out of our end zone." Her prayers were answered when three passes fell incomplete. State was reeling and we were rowdy. Sansing looked every bit the Roman emperor cheering on his legions, wispy white hair blowing in the wind. Borne was so hoarse he might have been yelling underwater. Shapiro looked like the wrath of Jehovah. A fourth down pass fell incomplete and I started to light a Cuban cigar. Dean tugged at my sleeve. A pass interference call had given State a first down at the Rebel one yardline. "Four more tries?" we asked each other in stunned horror, while some of the Bulldog fans actually clucked in sympathy.

In his grey overcoat Barry Hannah had the stonelike concentration of Rodin's "The Thinker." Having lost her voice Dean could only whisper, "De-fense, de-fense!" For an eternity we watched a goalline stand that Billy Brewer later declared impossible. Four more times the Rebels held—against two thrusts into the line, a quarterback bootleg alertly sniffed out by strong safety Johnny Dixon and All-SEC linebacker

THE HIT: Defensive tackle Chad Brown dumps the ballcarrier for a loss while quarterback Plump looks on in disbelief.

BRUCE NEWMAN

ABOVE: Safety Michael Lowery's interception ended State's first series inside the Rebel ten-yard line.

Dewayne Dotson, and then, finally, Greg Plump's desperation pass which State's receiver almost caught.

Like a priest giving final absolution Russ Shows took the last snap, knelt to the ground and it was over. Ole Miss had beaten State at Vaught-Hemingway and was Liberty Bowl-bound.

Of all the things that matter, birth and death and forgiveness and humility and hope and love, what else could have made us weep and laugh and grasp the hands of strangers in red and blue? We were one tribe, one nation, indivisible, with victory and glad tidings for all. At the other end of the field, Ole Miss students were

tearing down the goalposts yet the south end zone would endure a more subtle pillage. As writers and artists exchanged high-fives and praise both Biblical and secular, Dean and Jane Rule slipped onto the field and devoutly tore up a piece of lime-streaked turf, now enshrined in our kitchen window with Weems's Haitian cross embedded in it. Underneath it is a motto from Alexander the Great: "One moment without fear makes a man immortal." I leaned over the railing and thought, "But isn't football only a game?" And the walls of Vaught-Hemingway resounded with the celestial voices of Bruiser Kinard,

Tad Smith and Merle Hapes, now
scrimmaging with the SEC
Immortals under Coach Bear
Bryant, speaking to bum and emper-
or alike:

   Satisfaction is no game.

Lettermen

Season Records

Ole Miss Lettermen

Since 1893

A

Abdo, Nicholas, QB, 1927
Abide, Gary, LB, 1989-90-91-92
Ables, Winifred Wayne, mgr., 1980
Adamcik, Rich, OT, 1986; OG, 1987
Adams, Billy Ray, FB, 1959-60-61
Adams, J. C., C, 1909-10-11-12-(c)
Adams, Lawrence, QB, 1992
Adams, Robert O. (Tiger), E, 1952-53-54
Adams, Winfred C., sub-RG, 1908-09
Ainsworth, Stephen Gregory, TB, 1970-71-72
Akin, Wm. E. (Dooley), FB, 1921-22-23-24
Albritton, Sam, DT, 1984
Aldridge, John B., DT, 1968-69-70
Aldridge, Walter P. (Bo), T, 1962-63-64
Alexander, Charles H., Jr., mgr., 1972
Alexander, George E., E, 1920-21
Alexander, Jud, OG, 1983-84; OG-C, 1985
Alexander, Raymond M., DE, 1974
Alford, John Warner, LG, 1958-59-60-(co-c)
Allen, Charles B., FB-QB, 1923-24-25
Allen, Elmer Dale, ST, 1969; DT, 1970-71
Allen, Herman Eugene, FB, 1971-72-73
Allen, John Franklin, G, 1981-82-83
Alliston, George B., G, 1966
Alliston, Vaughn S., Jr. (Buddy), LG, 1953-54-55-(c)
Ambrose, J. R., SE, 1984-85, FL, 1986-87
Ames, Charles F., C-T, 1901-02
Amos, Dwayne, WR-DB, 1988; RB, 1989; CB, 1990-91-92
Amsler, Guy, G, 1920
Anderson, Cephus, C, 1913-14, 1916-(c)
Anderson, James N., FB, 1958-59-60
Anderson, Vernon, mgr., 1941
Applewhite, Austin H., E, 1925-26-27-(c)
Armstrong, Crowell H., LB, 1969-70-71
Armstrong, George W., T, 1923-24
Armstrong, Johnny, DB, 1981-82-83-84
Armstrong, Tyji, TE, 1990-91
Arnette, J. W., T, 1944
Arnold, John Wes, Jr., mgr., 1966
Arnold, Robert P., LB, 1972; DE, 1973-74
Arrington, Perry, C, 1988-89
Ashford, Andre L., trainer, 1972
Ashley, Tyrone, SE, 1989; FL-DB, 1990; RB-DB, 1991
Aston, Vernon (Monk), C, 1935-36-37
Austin, Kent, QB, 1981-82-83-84-85
Austin, Oliver A., mgr., 1910
Autrey, Winkey, C, 1937-38-39
Ayers, Chris, mgr., 1989
Ayers, Richardson, C, 1908

B

Bacon, Jeff, LB, 1984-85-86
Bagwell, C. I., T, 1917-18
Bagwell, Michael Wm., WB, 1970
Bailess, Robert R. (Bob), LB, 1971-72-73
Bailey, Jay Alan, LB, 1978
Bailey, Robert W., M, 1966-67-68-(co-c)
Baker, Jerry E., FB-RHB, 1954-55-56
Baldwin, Randy, RB, 1989-90
Ball, John, HB, 1914; 1916
Ball, Warren N. (Bo), E, 1958-59-60
Bane, Bob, mgr., 1977
Barber, John T., RH, 1954
Barbour, Calvin C., Jr., HB-QB, 1919-20-21-22-(c)
Barfield, Kenneth A., T, 1950-51
Barker, Reuben A. (Rube), T, 1911-12
Barkley, William Donald, LE, 1955, 1957
Barlow, Bobby, trainer, 1985-86
Barlow, T. Michael, TB, 1974
Barnes, Blake, mgr., 1977
Barnett, Eddie Lee, G, 1967
Barry, Wm. T. (Bill), FLK, 1971-72
Bartling, McNeil (Doby), QB, 1934-35
Basham, Wm. Earl, T-G, 1959-60-61
Baskin, John Frank, DT, 1969
Bates, G. C., RT-LG, 1905-06
Batten, H. C., FB, 1926
Battiste, Chris, OG, 1992
Baumsten, Herb, QB-FB, 1935-36-37
Beanland, Gayle C., QB, 1898-99, 1902
Beatty, Edwin M., C, 1951-52-53-(c)
Beck, John Robert, LB, 1976-77
Beckett, B. B., LE, 1901
Beckett, George B., LE, 1900
Beckett, Richard C., Jr., RE, 1905

Beddenfield, Marcus, E, 1934
Beddingfield, Wm. Ray, C, 1963-64-65
Bell, J. H., HB, 1914
Bell, Jeffrey D., trainer, 1980
Bell, Jonathan, FB, 1992
Bell, Tim, trainer, 1980-81-82
Bender, Charles A., FB, 1913-14
Bennett, Gardner, G, 1937
Bennett, Preston (Pep), QB, 1940-41, 1946
Bennett, Tony, DE, 1986; NG, 1987; OLB, 1988-89 (co-c)
Bentley, M. C., G, 1929
Benton, Robert Hollis, RT, 1958-59-60
Benvenutti, Joseph D., DT, 1974
Bernard, Dave, FB-HB, 1934-35-36
Bernocci, Robert, T, 1940-41-42
Berry, Lance, K, 1992
Berry, O. L., mgr., 1925
Berryhill, Herman, E, 1934
Besselman, Jim, OG, 1986; OT, 1987
Bethay, Kenneth Lee, trainer, 1980
Bevill, Scott, mgr., 1988
Bidgood, Charles S., C, 1947-48
Biggers, Neal B., HB, 1929-30-31-(c)
Bigham, C. S., sub., 1908
Bilbo, G. W., E-G, 1931-32-33
Bilbo, J. P., G, 1935-36-37
Biles, George Lacey, HB, 1924-25-26
Billings, Darron, FB, 1988 RB, 1990-91 (co-c)
Bingham, Dwight, DE, 1982-83-84
Bisbing, Willard, LH, 1938
Bishop, Clark D., E, 1949
Bishop, Smith, T, 1913-14
Black, Willis W., HB, 1954
Blackwell, Anse, E, 1938
Blackwell, Bernard, LG, 1944-45-46-47
Blair, Earl E., LHB, 1952-53-54-55
Blair, George L., LHB, 1958-59-60
Blair, Wiley S., sub., 1905
Blake, Walter G., RG, 1893-94
Blakemore, Robert E., DE, 1980-81;
    DT, 1983-84-(co-c)
Blalack, Charley, mgr., 1956
Blalack, John W., QB, 1954-55-56
Blankenbaker, R. H., HB-G, 1926-27-28
Blount, Clayton, HB, 1946
Blount, Joseph L., LB, 1967-68-69
Blount, Kenneth Lloyd, S, 1970
Boatman, Johnny, FB, 1985-86
Bogard, Harold, E, 1935
Boggan, Rex Reed, RT, 1949-50, 1954
Bolin, Treva (Bookie), RG, 1960-61
Bonham, Vince, C, 1988-89
Bontrager, Thomas, trainer, 1984-85
Bookout, B. E., HB, 1917
Boone, James T. (Pete), C, 1970-71-72
Booth, Carl C., III (Cliff), MG, 1968
Boothe, R. V., sub., 1893
Bounds, Wayne Stanley, QB, 1973, 1975
Bourdeaux, R. H., sub., 1893
Bourne, Robert, G, 1961
Boutwell, George, C, 1928-29-30
Bowen, B. C., RT, 1898
Bowen, John H., Jr. (Buddy), QB, 1946-47-48
Bowen, John H., III (Bo), TB, 1967; FB, 1968-69-(co-c)
Bowen, Mark Sutton, SE, 1976
Bowers, S. H., QB, 1919
Bowles, Wallace C., T-G, 1929-30-31
Bowman, Gayle, HB, 1955
Boyce, Boykin, G, 1944-45
Boyce, Daniel, OG, 1983; LB, 1984-85
Boyd, Danny, CB, 1989-90-91-92
Boyd, Lucas, mgr., 1953
Boyd, Robert C. (Bobby), QB, 1962
Boykin, A. L. (Showboat), HB-FB, 1949-50-51
Bradley, Bruce B., LH, 1949-50
Bradley, Kimble, QB, 1936-37-38-(c)
Brady, T. P., LT, 1893
Brandon, Gary, mgr., 1978
Brandon, Ronnie, mgr., 1980
Brashier, Rodgers, G, 1952-53-54
Breland, Hugh Gregory, P, 1973-74
Breland, J. J., FB-HB, 1912-13
Breland, R. Q., mgr., 1923
Brenner, George, FB, 1950-51-52
Brents, Darrel, C, 1944

Bressler, Arthur, Jr., (Art), OG, 1971-72-73
Brewer, Brett, P, 1984
Brewer, Derek O., DB, 1980
Brewer, Grady, FB, 1945
Brewer, Jack, E, 1944
Brewer, Joe, G, 1981-83; LB-1984; NG, 1985
Brewer, John Lee, RE, 1957, 1959-60
Brewer, William E., QB, 1957-58-59
Breyer, Alex, G, 1934-35-36
Brice, Alundis, FS, 1991-92
Bridgers, David I., C, 1946-47
Bridgers, David I., Jr., C, 1968; WG, 1969-70
Bridgers, James T., E, 1951-52
Bridgers, Lloyd M., mgr., 1975
Bridges, Roy, QB, 1917-(c)
Briggs, Charles E., mgr., 1924
Brinkley, Lester, DT, 1985-86-87-88
Brister, Fred E., III, LB, 1968-69-70
Brister, Herndon, FB, 1930
Brister, Thomas S., RE, 1961
Britt, Alvin, C-G, 1931-32-33
Britt, Oscar, G, 1940-41-42
Broussard, Ken G., T, 1965
Brown, Allen, E., 1962-63-64-(co-c)
Brown, Alton L., DT, 1971-72
Brown, Burkes, OT, 1991-92
Brown, Carter, HB, 1952
Brown, Chad, DL, 1991-92 (co-c)
Brown, Colon, HB, 1929-30
Brown, Dean, SE, 1983-85
Brown, Ernest Herman, S, 1970; SLB, 1971
Brown, Fred, G, 1946
Brown, Jerry G., T, 1959-60-61
Brown, Melvin A., RB, 1979; CB, 1980-81-82
Brown, Patrick, LB, 1982-83-84-85
Brown, Raymond L., QB, 1955-56-57
Brown, Renard, FB, 1992
Brown, Tim, OG, 1988-89 (co-c)
Brown, Titus, FL, 1986
Brown, Tony, OLB, 1990-91
Brown, Wm. Van., WB, 1967; KS, 1968
Brownlee, Vincent, WR, 1990-91
Bruce, John, QB, 1944-45
Buchanan, John P., DE, 1974
Buchanan, Oscar, T, 1944
Buchanan, Oscar W. (Red), QB, 1946-47-48
Buntin, R. R., 1915-16
Burford, Cecil, trainer, 1983-84
Burgess, G. Bentley, DE, 1980
Burke, Charles G., Jr., LE, 1955, 1957
Burke, Jack, HB, 1931-32
Burke, Webster W., C, 1924-25-26-(c)
Burke, Robert O., Jr., WT, 1969-70; QT, 1971
Burkhalter, Charles Stephen (Steve), DT,
    1971-72-73

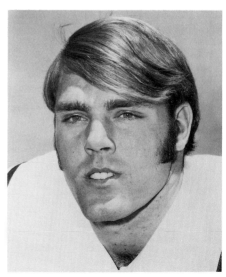

Floyd Franks, All-SEC Split End

Burleson, Charles, T, 1952
Burnett, Harvey, QB, 1930
Burnett, W. D. (Dump), T-G-FB, 1927-28-29-(c)
Burns, Willie, CB, 1977-78
Burrow, John D., DB, 1979-80-81; FS, 1982
Bush, Alan L., ST, 1965-66-67
Bush, Bill, OG, 1989; DL, 1991
Butler, George H., LG, 1900
Butler, James, G, 1944
Byrd, Ronard K. (Rocky), QB, 1949-50-51

C

Caccamo, Dan, SS, 1977-78-79
Cage, Charlie, Jr., DT, 1976-77-78
Cagle, Brian, DT, 1988; DE, 1989; DT, 1990
Cagle, Robert, OG, 1987
Cahall, William C., QB, 1911
Cain, George, FS, 1977
Cairnes, George H., sub., 1899-1900
Caldwell, David, FS, 1985; SE, 1987
Caldwell, James T., LG, 1950-51-52
Caldwell, M. F., T, 1917
Calhoun, Bill, trainer, 1984-85
Callahan, Lindy T., HB, 1949-50-51
Campanova, Joseph F., KS, 1980
Campbell, David, DB, 1977
Campbell, Eugene P., RG-mgr., 1898-(c), 1899
Campbell, Henry A., G, 1948
Campbell, Jeff, T, 1982-83
Campbell, J. W., FB, 1916
Campbell, Keith, CB, 1992

Bobby Crespino, halfback

Campbell, William Mike, E, 1945
Cannon, Glenn D., S, 1967-68-69-(co-c)
Cantrell, James Larry, OT, 1975
Capello, Harry, C, 1940
Carlisle, Wm. Todd, mgr., 1968
Carlson, Cully, E, 1935
Carlton, John, DT, 1985, 1987
Carnes, Robert Lee, E, 1954
Carney, A. B., QB, 1918-19
Carpenter, Charles W. (Chuck), OG, 1971
Carpenter, Preston Caswell, TE, 1969; DE, 1970-71
Carpenter, Terry Carol, WB, 1967
Carr, Oscar, E, 1914
Carruth, Bert, FS, 1991-92
Carruth, Lester, G, 1932-33-34
Carter, Fred S., LG-T, 1909-10-11
Carter, Jeff, DB, 1988; FS, 1989-90-91 (co-c)
Carter, Raymond, G, 1965
Carter, Sam P., G-C, 1929-30
Carter, W. Spinks, C, 1901
Case, Harry, E, 1956
Casper, Raymond, QB-HB, 1931-32-33
Castle, C. E., HB, 1945
Castle, Lee, FB, 1941
Castle, Richard, HB, 1945
Caston, Lester B. (Brent), TB, 1964; M, 1965-66
Causey, J. B., LT-G, 1909-10-11
Causey, Jimmy, S, 1971; QB, 1972
Cavin, Jack Ottis, RE, 1958

Chamberlain, D. H., LH, 1904
Champion, James E., HB, 1957-58-59
Champion, Wm. L. (Billy), LE, 1960, 1962
Chandler, John Caroll, LB, 1970-71-72
Chandler, Kyle, RH, 1899
Cheatham, Jack, G, 1945
Childers, Charles, P, 1987-88-89-90
Childres, Robert D., HB, 1952-53
Chisholm, Charles P., TB, 1964
Chisolm, Richard, P, 1991-92
Christian, Charles D., Jr., RH, 1907
Chumbler, Brent S. (Shug), QB, 1969-70-71
Chunn, Clifton B., Jr., (Cliff), DHB, 1968
Churchwell, Hanson (Bull), RG-T, 1957-58
Clapp, Robert P., QB, 1899
Clark, Bobby, OG, 1982-83-84-85
Clark, James H., T, 1944, 1947-48-49
Clark, Marcus R. (Mark), FLK, 1976
Clark, Roger Lamar, DB, 1981-82-83
Clay, Wm. F. (Bill), WB-DHB, 1963-64-65
Cleveland, Chuck, TB, 1985; FB, 1986-87
Clippard, Ricard F., OG, 1973-74; MG, 1975
Coates, David Patrick, QB, 1976-77
Cobb, Shawn, LB, 1987-88-89-90 (co-c)
Cohen, Sollie, FB, 1925-26-27
Cohn, Abye A., HB, 1901; 1903-04
Cohn, Henry L., RG-Mgr., 1909-10-11-12
Coker, Wm. H. (Billy), WG, 1968-69-70
Cole, Alfred Lee, LB, 1980-81-82-83
Cole, Eddie Lee, LB, 1975-76-77-78
Cole, Milton R. (Hoppy), NG, 1980; G, 1981-82
Coleman, Dennis F., DE, 1968-69-70-(co-c)
Coleman, Kem T., LB, 1974-75-76-77
Coleman, Pat, FL, 1988-89 (co-c)
Coleman, Roy, FLK, 1977; QB, 78-79
Collette, Allen, G, 1914-15
Collier, Antonio, FS, 1992
Collier, J. H., 1895
Collier, John Brooks, DT, 1969
Collier, O. E., HB, 1926
Collier, Terry Lee, QB, 1967
Collier, William C., sub., 1893
Collins, Dudley, mgr., 1931
Commiskey, Chuck C., 1977, 79-80
Conerly, Cecil (Chip), mgr., 1977
Conerly, Charles A., LHB, 1942, 1946-47-(c)
Conlee, Clint, OT, 1990-91-92
Conn, Abe H., FB, 1898, 1901
Conner, Clyde R., T, 1902, 1906
Conner, Edgar E., RT, 1901
Conroy, James, HB, 1944
Cook, Richard, HB, 1925
Cook, William Henry, FB, 1893-94-(c)
Cooper, Charles, T, 1945
Cooper, Harold, LG, 1956-57-58
Cooper, Kyle M., LE, 1907
Correro, Van Sam, OG, 1973-74
Cothren, Jennings Paige, FB, 1954-55-56
Cottam, Chris C., OT, 1978-79-80
Courtney, Marvin, RB, 1990-91-92
Cowan, John Kuhl, RT, 1893-94
Cowan, R. C., RT, 1901
Coward, Charles B., LB, 1967
Cowart, E. M., E, 1917-18-19-(c)
Cox, Owen E., G, 1950
Crain, Milton, C, 1956-57-58-(co-c)
Crain, Sollie M., T-G, 1921-22-23-24
Crawford, Edward S., III, LHB, 1954-55-56
Crawford, James A., RG, 1946-47-48-49
Crawford, Othar A., Jr., LG, 1947, 1949-50-51-(c)
Creekmore, Rufus H., T-C, 1918-19-20-(c)
Crespino, Robert, RHB, 1958-59-60
Crisman, William O., LH, 1900-01-02
Critz, F. A., Jr., RH-LH, 1900, 1902
Crocker, W. David, TE, 1974
Crook, G. W., FB, 1920
Crook, Jerry, HB, 1945
Crosby, William F. (Buddy), HB, 1961-62
Crowder, Talbert, T, 1937
Crowe, Dorman, C, 1938
Crull, Luther P., Jr. (Putt), MG, 1968
Cunningham, Julian D. (Doug), TB, 1964-66-(co-c); WB, 1965
Cunningham, James W., LH-sub., 1905-06
Cunningham, Stephen Vincent, RB, 1981; CB, 1982; FL, 1983; CB, 1984
Curd, H. P., mgr., 1919
Curland, Marvin, FB, 1946
Curlee, R. M., RG, 1900
Curtis, Chester, HB, 1932-33-34
Curtis, J. E., HB, 1915

D

Dabbs, Willis N. (Woody), RE, 1960-61-62
Dale, Roland H., C, 1945; T, 1947-48-49-(c)
Dalton, Andy, trainer, 1988-89-90
Dalton, Anthony D., DT, 1979-80; G, 1981-82
Daly, Jerome, HB, 1942
Daniels, Jerry S., E, 1958-59-60

Dantzler, Larry D., LB, 1974-75; DE, 1976; LB, 1977
Darby, Al, trainer, 1982
Darnell, John, QB, 1987-88-89 (co-c)
Davenport, Butch, DB, 1985; CB, 1986-87; FS, 1988
Davidson, J. W., E, 1939-40-41-(co-c)
Davidson, P. G., E, 1919-20
Davis, Curtis Reed, LE, 1961-62-63
Davis, Edwin D., T, 1929-30
Davis, Frank, HB, 1945
Davis, Frank O., RHB, 1900
Davis, Harry, HB, 1949-50
Davis, J. E., E, 1923-24
Davis, Lee Andrew, CB, 1981-83-84
Davis, Mark, mgr., 1983
Davis, Paul, C, 1942, 1946
Davis, Richie, NG, 1986-87
Davis, Robert, T, 1924-25-26
Davis, Shed H., T, 1921-22-23-24
Davis, Steve, QB, 1990-91
Davis, Thomas D., RH-sub., 1899, 1900
Dawson, D. A., HB, 1915
Day, Charles, T, 1940
Day, Herman (Eagle), QB, 1953-54-55
Day, William Glynn, LCB, 1976-77-78
Dean, Guy D., FB, 1901-02
Dean, Wm. J. (Joe), LT, 1962-63-64
Dear, W. C., HB, 1913, 1915
Dearie, Steven Patrick, TE, 1981
Deaton, Daniel B. (Penny), SE, 1969
Denmark, Eric, T, 1983-84
Dennis, Walter M. (Mike), TB, 1963-64-65-(co-c)
Denny, Billy, TE, 1977-78-79
Dent, Edward L., RG, 1903
Dentley, Tony, FB, 1986
Dew, Cliff, C, 1990-91
Dickens, Luther (Curley), T, 1934-35-36
Dickerson, Cecil R., HB, 1946
Dickerson, David L., E, 1952-53-54
Dickey, Bubba, LB, 1985-86-87; OG, 1988
Dickson, Donald, RG, 1960-61-62
Dill, John Reginald (Reggie), LB, 1970; DE, 1971-72-(co-c)
Dill, Kenneth D., C, 1961-62-63-(co-c)
Dillard, Wilson, Jr., HB, 1950-51-52
Dillingham, Bruce, Jr., DHB, 1965-66-67
Dixon, Johnny, CB, 1990; SS, 1991-92
Dodd, Allen P., LG-LT, 1902-03-04-05-(c)
Dodson, Leslie, HB-FB, 1938-39-40
Dongieux, Paul A., LB, 1969-70-71-(co-c)
Dorrah, Clinton E., 1913
Dossett, Horace, T, 1938-39-40
Dotson, Albert C., CB, 1976-77
Dotson, Dwayne, LB, 1992
Dotson, G., Kenneth, DT, 1980-81-82
Dotson, Leslie, HB-FB, 1938-39-40
Dottley, John, FB, 1947-48-49-50
Doty, Arthur W., LH, 1960-61
Dowell, Wade, C, 1977
Downing, H. M., sub., 1903
Doyle, L. A., 1918
Drewry, Robert G., 1953-54-55
Dubuisson, Gene H., C, 1953-54-55
Duck, Charles E., G, 1955-56
Duke, John Gayle, QB, 1894
Dunagin, Charles Ado, T, 1937-38-39
Dunaway, James K., RT, 1960-61-62
Duncan, Derek, mgr., 1983-84
Duncan, Sam, trainer, 1978
Dunn, Perry Lee, QB, 1961-63; FB, 1962
Dunn, Thomas, HB, 1931
Durfey, Allan P., HB, 1918
Dykes, Jewell Kenny, Jr., mgr., 1968

E

East, F. J., G, 1915
Easterling, Jay, KS, 1979
Easton, Mike, OT, 1989
Edwards, Arthur M., trainer, 1975
Ellis, Timothy L. (Tim), QB, 1974-75-76-77
Elmer, Frederick W., RE-RH-mgr., 1900-01-(c); 1902-03-(c); 1904
Elmer, James C., RT, 1906
Elmore, James Douglas, QB, 1959-60-61-(t-c)
Elmore, J. W., 1924
English, Gino D., FLK, 1980-81-82
Enoch, Eugene S., QB-sub., 1900-01-02
Enochs, W. B., C, 1926-27
Epting, John Booth, HB, 1922
Erickson, W. C. (Bill), T, 1946-47-(alt-c)
Erves, Dale V., LB, 1979-80; FB, 1981
Erves, James C., DT, 1979-80
Erwin, Clay, DE, 1977, 1980-81
Estes, Hermon Donald, mgr., 1964
Estes, Terry, mgr., 1970
Eubanks, Bill, LE, 1940-41
Eubanks, O. G., 1921
Evans, Guy E. (Butch), QB, 1974; DE, 1975
Evans, Harrison, G, 1916
Evans, J. P. (Joe), E-QB, 1912-13-14

Jim Dunaway, All-America tackle

F

Fabris, Jon Michael, FS, 1976-77; CB, 1978-79
Fabris, Robert S., TE, 1975; SE, 1976-77
Fagan, Julian W., III, P, 1967-68-69
Fair, Davis L., LG, 1901
Fair, Frank L., LE, 1903
Fair, Gene, mgr., 1937
Fant, Frank C., G, 1947-48-49
Farber, Louis A. (Hap), SE, 1967; DE, 1968-69
Farish, William S., RT-FB, 1899
Farmer, C. E., G, 1918-19
Farmer, Fred R., DHB, 1968-69-70
Farmer, James J., T, 1966-67
Farragut, Kenneth D., C, 1947-48-49-50-(c)
Farrar, Donald H. (Don), QB, 1968, 1970
Farris, Wm. J. (Bill), DE, 1973-74-75
Fraser, D. R., mgr., 1928
Fedric, Jones, mgr., 1932
Feemster, J. H., T, 1919-20; 1922
Felts, Morris Leon, TB, 1968-69; SE, 1971
Ferguson, David, trainer, 1988-89
Ferrill, Charles, C, 1931
Ferrill, Charles B., RT, 1960
Fields, Jimmy, NG, 1985
Fields, Richard J., HB, 1917
Finger, William, G, 1915
Finley, J. A., FB-QB, 1904-05
Fischer, David M. (Danny), FLK, 1976
Fisher, Bobby F., LE, 1954-55
Fitzsimmons, Mike, NG, 1983; DT, 1984-85-86
Flack, Jackie, LH, 1940-41
Flakes, Everett, DB, 1984; SS, 1985-86
Fleming, Gordon W., Jr. (Rocky), LE, 1964-65; WB, 1966
Fletcher, Ralph E., QB, 1912
Fletcher, Robert J., E, 1947-48-49-50
Fletcher, Spence, trainer, 1988-89
Flowers, Charles, FB, 1957-58-59-(co-c)
Flowers, Jesse, T, 1931-32-33
Foose, Sam, E, 1935
Forbes, George, trainer, 1988
Ford, Artis, DL, 1990-91-92
Ford, Cecil A., RT, 1961-62-63
Forester, Michael W., C, 1974; DT, 1975-76
Foster, John M., LE-RH, 1898-99-1900-01-02-(c)
Foster, Willie, FLK, 1978
Fountain, Michael A., CB, 1978-79-80
Fourcade, John, Jr., QB, 1978-79-80-81
Fourcade, Keith J., LB, 1979-80-81-82
Fowler, Ronald M. (Ronnie), C-G, 1964-65-66
Foxworth, T. J., QB, 1893
Frame, J. S. (Buntin), DHB, 1965
Franklin, Bobby Ray, QB, 1957-58-59
Franks, Floyd W., SE, 1968-69-70
Franks, Michael Dwayne, TB-SE, 1970; DHB, 1971
Fraser, D. R., mgr., 1928
Fratesi, Michael L. (Mickey), S, 1971; M, 1972; SS, 1973
Freightman, Phil, S, 1978-79
Friedrichsen, Mark, T, 1982-83
Frishman, Leon B., mgr., 1967
Frye, J. P., G, 1940-41
Frye, William, FB, 1937

Fuerst, Robert J., G, 1946, 1948-49
Fulton, Lyman A., mgr., 1981
Funderburk, Joe, T, 1915
Furlow, Frank, QB, 1940

G

Gaddis, J. T., HB, 1913
Galey, Charles D., E, 1945-46-47
Gallik, Gerald, OT-C, 1985, OT, 1986
Gardner, Robert L. (Bobby), QB, 1976-77-78-(c)
Gardner, Thomas, mgr., 1938
Gardner, William P., G, 1919
Gardner, Wm. Douglas, G, 1932
Garner, Ernest L., Jr. (Lee), FB, 1964; LB, 1965-66
Garner, John C., Jr., DE, 1968
Garnett, C. L., 1895
Garrigues, Robert M., DHB, 1966-67-68
Gartrell, J. E., LT, 1900
Gary, Oscar Knox, Jr., LG, 1951-52
Gates, Hunter, G, 1946
Gatlin, Todd E., KS, 1980-81-82
Gazelle, J. J., HB, 1922
Gebbia, Rich, TE, 1988-89
Genovese, Ross, OT-C, 1984-85
George, Alonzo P., G-HB, 1917; 1919-20
Gerrard, Albert L., Jr. (Bud), C, 1945; 1949
Gibbs, Jerry D. (Jake), QB, 1958-59-60-(co-c)
Gibson, E. B., 1895
Gibson, Jonathan, OG, 1992
Gilbert, Kline, E-T, 1950-51-52-(co-c)
Gill, Virgil, T, 1932-33-34
Gilliland, John L., DE, 1968-69-70
Gilruth, I. Newton, LE-RT, 1899-1900
Gipson, Malvin, TB, 1978; DB, 1979; TB, 1980-81
Gladding, Charles, E, 1939
Glover, Will H., LH, 1947
Gober, Oscar, 1921
Godwin, Chauncey, DB, 1988; CB, 1989-90-91
Goehe, Richard, RT, 1953-54-55
Goff, Rob, C, 1986-87
Goodloe, Willie, TB, 1984-85-86-87
Goodwin, Arthur, LE, 1940
Gordon, Craig, mgr., 1982
Gordon, J. O., G, 1919
Gordon, Louis, LB, 1988; OLB, 1989; TE, 1990
Gordon, Roger, FB, 1977
Gourley, John, trainer, 1991-92
Graeber, Jerry, SS, 1992
Graham, Bonnie Lee, E, 1936-37-38
Graham, Darryl E., P, 1980-81-82
Graham, Michael F. (Mike), SE, 1965
Grant, Roy Oliver, OG-T, 1975; OG, 1976
Grantham, James Larry, LE, 1957-58-59
Graves, Joe E. (Jody), QB, 1965-66
Graves, Sam Ervin, III, LB, 1966-67
Gray, Brad, P, 1991-92
Gray, Dabney, mgr., 1969
Green, Allen L., C, 1958-59-60
Green, Jonathan, CB, 1991
Green, Marcus, DT, 1982-83-84
Green, Norvin E., C, 1900
Green, Walter G., HB, 1912
Green, Willie, WR, 1986-87; SE, 1988-89
Greene, James M., Jr., MG, 1979
Greenich, Harley, HB-FB, 1940; 1942
Greenlee, Max H., LT, 1964
Greenlee, Phillip Murry, FS, 1973
Grefseng, Robert Leonard (Bob), DE, 1976-77-78
Gregory, George H., Jr., E, 1958
Gregory, John Andrew, OT, 1970-71-72
Griffin, J. A., HB-E, 1914-15
Griffin, Wade H., OT, 1974; TE, 1975-76-(co-c)
Griffin, William K., KS, 1976
Griffing, Glynn, QB, 1960-61-62-(co-c)
Grigg, Jack Norwood, DT, 1979-80
Gryder, Robert L., Trnr., 1978
Gunn, Edgar Lindsey, mgr., 1972
Gunn, Lundy R., TE, 1973-74
Gunter, Bubba, OLB, 1988-89
Gunter, George, FB-HB, 1932-33-34
Guy, Louis B., WB, 1960-61-62-(co-c)

H

Haddock, James W., S, 1965; 1967
Haik, Joseph Michel (Mac), SE, 1965-66-67-(co-c)
Halbert, Frank R., RH-FB, 1960-61
Hall, Gary S., SE, 1972; RCB, 1973; FS, 1974
Hall, J. J., 1921
Hall, J. P., LT, 1899
Hall, James S., LH, 1957-58-59
Hall, Joe, DB, 1982-83
Hall, Linus Parker, HB, 1936-37-38
Hall, Wm. Whaley, LT, 1961-62-63-(co-c)
Hamilton, William F., RCB, 1976
Hamley, Douglas, T, 1946-47-48-(c); 1949
Hamley, Stuart Douglas, Jr., TB, 1973

Hancock, Roger, SS, 1987; DB, 1988; SS, 1989; OLB, 1990
Hannah, Otis, 1928
Hapes, Clarence, T-FB, 1934-35-36
Hapes, Merle, FB, 1939-40-41
Hapes, Ray, HB, 1935-36-37
Haralson, M. Flint, G, 1912
Harbin, Leon C., Jr. (Buddy), E, 1954-55-56
Harbour, James E., SE, 1980-81; FL, 1982-84
Harbuck, Sonny, OG, 1985-86-87
Harden, Edwin D., mgr., 1973
Hardy, Wm. H., Jr., sub., 1903
Harmon, Michael, FLK, 1979-80-81-82
Harper, Anthony Keith, TE, 1981-82
Harper, Brian, DL, 1991
Harper, Everette L., E, 1945-46-47
Harris, Antonio, TB, 1985
Harris, Dan D., Jr. (Danny), DHB, 1971; 1973
Harris, David, DL, 1991-92
Harris, George, E, 1952-53-54
Harris, I. H., FB, 1912
Harris, J. Harley (Pop), FB-T, 1913-14-15-(c)
Harris, James E., FB, 1974-75
Harris, Luther C. (Luke), DE, 1976
Harris, Pete, LB, 1988-89-90-91
Harris, R. S., mgr., 1916
Harris, Tony, DB, 1988
Harris, Wayne Stanley, WB, 1964
Harrison, Elvin Lee (Harry), S, 1971-72-73
Harrison, Glenn D., MG, 1968
Hart, Frank E., T, 1936-37-38
Hart, Granville W., LH, 1950
Harthcock, Billy Harold, WB, 1966-67
Hartzog, Hugh Miller, Jr., MG, 1967-68; DT, 1969
Harvey, Addison, LH, 1899
Harvey, Fernando C., LT, 1976-77-78
Harvey, James B., RT, 1963-64-65
Hatch, Johnny A., CB, 1974
Hathcock, Lance, DG, 1984-85, NG, 1986
Hathorn, Samuel C., LE, 1909-10
Havard, Gerald W. (Scooter), FB, 1969-70
Havard, Richard J. (Rickey), TB, 1969-70-71
Hawkins, Jim, OT, 1977-78-79
Hawley, Mike, mgr., 1984
Haxton, R. Kenneth, QB-HB, 1909-10; 1912
Haynes, Kirk, HB, 1930-31-32
Hazel, Homer Lawrence, G, 1939-40-41-(co-c)
Hazel, William M., 1939-40-41
Heidel, James B., S-QB, 1963-64-65
Heidel, Herlan Ray, DHB, 1968-69-70
Heidel, Roy E., LE, 1963-64-65
Hemphill, Archie W., T-G, 1927-28
Hemphill, Robert E., HB, 1948-49
Hendrix, Robert E. Jr., WT, 1965-67; WG, 1966
Hendrix, Steven M., TE, 1980; G, 1981; FB, 1983
Henley, Tracy, trainer, 1982
Henry, Antonio, LB, 1990
Henry, Patrick, Jr., RE, 1898-99
Henry, Robert B., OG, 1975-76
Henson, Erwin D., E, 1916
Herard, Claude D., DT, 1967-68-69
Herring, David, C, 1990-91
Herring, Stephen C., G, 1979; C, 1980-81-82
Herrington, Bart, C-E, 1931-32-33
Herrington, John C., sub., 1903
Herrod, Jeff, LB, 1984-85-86-87-(co-c)
Herron, Lee, trainer, 1991-92
Hervey, Tony, DT, 1990
Hester, S. D., G, 1929
Hewes, Gaston, 1924
Hickerson, Robert Gene, RT, 1955-56-57-(co-c)
Hickerson, Willie Wayne, RG, 1957
Hickman, James E., OT, 1973; 75; OG, 1974
Hicks, Rickye Allen, TE, 1972; FS, 1975-76
Hightower, C. C., sub., 1905-06
Hill, Jody, LB, 1990-91-92
Hindman, Stanley C., RG, 1963-64-65-(co-c)
Hindman, Stephen H., TB, 1966-67-68
Hines, Reid, WR, 1986-87; FL, 1988-89
Hinton, Benjamin E., DE, 1975-76
Hinton, Charles R., C, 1964-65-66-(co-c)
Hinton, Cloyce M., KS, 1969-70-71
Hitt, Billy C., 1951-52
Hofer, Paul D., FB, 1972-73-74-75-(tri-c)
Hoff, A. S., HB, 1923-24
Hogue, Greg, P, 1987-88-89
Holcombe, James, OG, 1991-92
Holden, Allison, trainer, 1992
Holder, Jamie, FL, 1983-84-(co-c)-85-(co-c)
Holder, Jeffrey, SE, 1988-89-90
Holder, Owen H., WT, 1968
Holladay, Robert, TE, 1987
Holloway, A. J., Jr., HB, 1960-61-62
Holloway, Ernest D., E, 1913
Holman, William O., RG, 1900
Holston, John C., E, 1958
Hood, H. M., T, 1920
Hooker, Clyde, HB, 1944
Hooker, Danny L., S, 1968-69-70
Hooper, William K., Jr., FB, 1979-80; LB, 1981; RB, 1982
Hopkins, O. S., RG-FB, 1901-02

Hopkins, Thomas J., RG-LT, 1902-03
Hopson, Jay, FS, 1988; SS, 1989-90-91
Horn, Jeffrey L., MG, 1968-69-70
Horne, James H., LB, 1971; 1973
Horne, Steve, mgr., 1985-86
Hoskins, Danny, OG, 1984-85-86-87
Houchins, L. Larry, mgr., 1974
Householder, Eddy, LB, 1977-78-79
Hovater, Nobel Owen, RT, 1964
Hovious, John A. (Junie), HB, 1939-40-41
Howard, Jon, K, 1984-85
Howell, Earl O. (Dixie), HB, 1947-48
Howell, J. M., HB, 1920
Howell, L. F., T, 1918
Howell, Ray, Jr., E, 1950-51-52
Hubbard, Ethelbert J., LH, 1898
Hubbard, Thomas Leon, LB, 1981-82-83
Huddleston, Quinnis (Fuzzy), LB, 1983-84-85-86
Hudson, Clark, 1979
Huff, Earl, T, 1955
Huff, Kenneth A., C, 1973
Huff, Tim, Trnr., 1978
Huff, Walter W., NG, 1980; T, 1981
Huggins, Cleveland P., RT-FB, 1904-05-06-(c)
Hughes, David, mgr., 1927
Humphrey, Arthur W., RB, 1981, FB, 1982-83-84
Humphrey, William R., G, 1950
Hunt, Kevin, mgr., 1988
Hurst, William Otis, FB, 1955-56-57
Hurt, Kevin, P, 1987
Hutchinson, James W., RE, 1898
Hutson, Earl, FB, 1932-33-34
Hutson, Marvin L., C, 1934-35-36-(c)

I

Ingram, James F., G-C, 1950-51-52-(co-c)
Ingram, Kevin, LB, 1990-91
Innocent, Dou, RB, 1991-92
Inzer, William H., B, 1929
Ireys, Junius Taylor, HB, 1894
Irvin, Todd, TE-OT, 1984; OT, 1985-86-87-(co-c)
Irwin, Billy Carl, LE, 1962-63-64

J

Jabour, Robert, QB, 1948-49-50
Jackson, Abdul, LB, 1991-92
Jackson, Antionne, DT, 1979
Jackson, Claude A. (Red), E, 1935-36
Jackson, Louis, DB, 1982
Jackson, Richard, LB, 1984
Jacobs, Doug, DT, 1988; DE, 1989; DT, 1990
James, Edward Thomas, Jr., DHB, 1965-66-67
James, James Elwyn, FB, 1969
James, Jerome P., G, 1913
James, Raymond L., LG, 1952-53-54
Jansen, Daniel J., RB, 1980-81-82

Jarman, Junius, 1924
Jarvis, Lewis Dewayne, TE, 1973-74
Jeanes, Kenneth L., DT, 1974
Jefcoat, Gregg, OG, 1978-79
Jenkins, Eulas S. (Red), FB, 1946-47-48-49
Jenkins, Robert L., QB, 1954
Jenkins, Warren D., RE, 1957-58
Jennings, David Sullivan, TB, 1962; 1964
Jennings, Steve, QB, 1977
Jennings, Thomas Wood, OT, 1975-76
Jernigan, Arthur F., Jr. (Skip), SG, 1968-69-70
Jernigan, Frank D., G, 1951-52-53
Jiggits, Louis M., HB, 1917; 1919
Johnson, Daren, FL, 1985, SE, 1986
Johnson, James L., C, 1901
Johnson, Joe C., E, 1944; 1947
Johnson, John, DT, 1977-78-79
Johnson, Larry Leo, WB, 1961-62-63
Johnson, Lawrence B., DT, 1974-75-77-78-(c)
Johnston, Hal G., RT-RG, 1907-08
Jones, Billy Ray, C-G, 1959-60-61-(tri-c)
Jones, Garland, RH, 1893
Jones, Gary M., FS, 1975-76-77
Jones, George F. (Buddy), WB, 1968-69-70
·Jones, Hermit, T, 1942
Jones, Jerrell, QB, 1941-42
Jones, Lopaz, DE, 1985-86-87; OLB, 1988
Jones, Robert H., G, 1928-29-30
Jones, S. M., LG, 1901
Jones, Walker W., III (Bill), TB, 1967; DHB, 1968-69
Jordan, James, MG, 1976-77-78-79
Jordan, Joel, OG, 1990-91-92
Jordan, Wm. Roberts (Bill), TE, 1970; FLK, 1972
Joyner, Steve, TE, 1983-84-85-86
Jumper, Zeke, E, 1927

K

Kanuch, Barry W., DE, 1978
Karliner, Randy, QB, 1992
Katzenmeyer, Fritz A., trainer, 1972
Kauerz, Don, T, 1945
Keaton, Grayson (Buster), G, 1921-22-23-24
Kelly, James A., FB-HB, 1951-52
Kemp, E. D., mgr., 1935
Kempinska, Charles C., RG-T, 1957-58-59
Kendall, Sam, C, 1915
Kennedy, Bryan G., DT, 1980; DE, 1981-82
Kent, Phillip, OLB, 1988-89-90-91 (co-c)
Kent, Robert W., mgr., 1972
Keyes, Jimmy Elton, MG, 1965-66; LB, 1967
Khayat, Robert C., T-G, 1957-58-59
Killam, John, T, 1944
Killion, Reed, LB, 1984-85
Kilpatrick, Wendell Terry, LB, 1972-73
Kimbrell, Fred T., Jr., C-LG, 1962
Kimbrough, Les, FLK, 1977-78
Kimbrough, Orman L., LE-LH-mgr., 1902-03; 1905

Kimbrough, Richard R. (Rick), FLK, 1973-74-75
Kimbrought, Thomas C., C, 1893-94
Kinard, Billy R., HB, 1952-53-54-55
Kinard, Frank M., T, 1935-36-37-(c)
Kinard, Frank M., Jr., FB, 1962-63-64
Kinard, George, G, 1938-39-40-(c)
Kinard, Henry L., 1938; 1940
Kincade, Robert, E, 1935-36-37
King, Derek, OG, 1986-87; OT, 1988
King, Derrick, LB, 1989-90-91-92
King, James, OG, 1986; OT, 1987; OG, 1988
King, Kenneth A., LB, 1973-74-(tri-c); 1975-(tri-c)
King, Michael L. (Mickey), C, 1969-70
King, Perry Lee, KS, 1968-69
King, Stark H., DE, 1966
Kinnebrew, Earl, RT, 1909-10
Kirk, Dixon, E, 1918
Kirk, Ken H., FB-C, 1957-58-59-(co-c)
Kirk, Robert D., DE, 1976
Kisner, Donald, mgr., 1978
Kitchens, Donald Scott, SLB, 1976-77
Knapp, C. E., HB, 1927-28
Knell, Doug, C, 1944
Knight, Wm. R. (Bob), DHB, 1969; TB, 1970-72
Knox, Baxter N., LT, 1908
Knox, Ike C., LH-RH, 1907-08-(c)
Knox, William W., III, DB, 1979-80-81-82
Kohn, Germaine, WR, 1991-92
Kota, Charles U. (Chuck), OG, 1975-76
Kozel, Chester, LT, 1939-40-41
Kramer, Larry E., TB, 1972-73-74
Kretschmar, W. P., E, 1896
Kroeze, John, P, 1986
Kyzer, Sam, HB, 1929-30

L

Laird, Charles D., FB, 1960
Laird, Dewitt, C, 1928
Lake, R. H., HB, 1918-19
Lamar, Wayne Terry, LG, 1959-60
Lambert, Sr., A. C. "Butch", mgr.-trnr., 1948
Lambert, Franklin T. (Frank), P, 1962-63-64
Lambert, George R., T, 1946
Lane, Paul J., Jr., QB, 1980; CB, 1981; RB, 1982
Langley, Carl Edward III (Hoppy),
    KS, 1976-77-78-79
Langston, Thomas E., T, 1950
Lanter, Lewis R., LE, 1961-62
Lantrip, Billy, OG, 1985
Lavinghouze, Robin C., KS, 1976-77
Lavinghouze, Stephen M., KS, 1972-73-74-75
Lawrence, Richard T. (Dick), OT,
    1973-74-(tri-c); 1975
Lawton, Pat, HB-mgr., 1929-30
Lea, Jim, trainer, 1985-86
Lear, James H., QB, 1950-51-52
Lear, Jim, QB, 1977-78-79

1954 SEC Champs

144

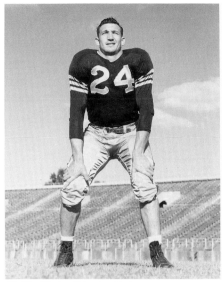

John "Kayo" Dottley, All-America tailback

Leathers, Don Wayne, OT, 1971-72-(co-c)
Leathers, W. S. (Dr.), mgr., 1902-03
Leavell, L. O., G, 1915
Leavell, Leonard, RG-LG, 1907-08
LeBlanc, Allen Michael, DE, 1969-70-71
Lee, Alonzo Church, FB, 1908-09-10
Lee, Brian, K, 1989-90-91-92
Lee, Greg, TE, 1986-87
Leftwich, Frank M., E, 1921-22-23
Leftwich, George J., FB, 1912
Leggett, Chuck, Tr., 1978
Lenhardt, John, FB, 1937
Lentjes, Fred W., C, 1959-60-61
Lentz, Jim, DT, 1988; NG, 1989-90-91
Lester, Victor, OLB, 1989-90
Lewis, Carl, LB, 1980; DE, 1981-82-83
Lewis, Robert Q. II, C, 1976-77
Lewis, Wm. Irwin (Buddy), C, 1966
Lillibridge, David B., E, 1916
Lilly, Sale T., HB, 1926-27
Lilly, T. J., HB, 1926
Lindsay, Derrick, FS, 1986-87
Lindsay, Everett, OT, 1989; OG, 1990-91;
   OT, 1992 (co-c)
Lindstrom, Ricky, LB, 1984
Linton, Henry, Jr., T, 1951-52-53
Little, Jamie Ray, E, 1964
Little, Robert (Robbie), WR, 1991
Lloyd, Donald J., TE, 1978-79-80
Lockhart, Walter W., sub., 1893
Lofton, Harol, HB-FB, 1951-52-53
Logan, Dameion, RB, 1991-92
Longest, Christopher C., LG, 1898-99-1900
Lorio, Franz, C, 1990-91-92
Lott, Billy Rex, RH, 1955-56-57
Lott, Lee, OT, 1988-89-90
Lotterhos, George T., DE, 1968-69-70
Lovelace, Kent E., HB, 1957-58
Lovelady, Matthew, LB, 1980; DT, 1981;
   DE, 1982-83
Lowe, Rodney, DT, 1985-86-87-88
Lowery, Michael, FS, 1992
Lucas, Thomas Edwin, RG, 1962; LT, 1964-65
Luke, Tom, QB, 1989-90-91
Luke, Tommy, DHB, 1964-65-66
Lumpkin, John, G, 1916
Lyell, G. Garland, mgr., 1897
Lyerly, Frank G., mgr., 1921
Lyles, Sam, G, 1938-39
Lyons, Kenneth J., Jr., 1971; 1973-74

Mc

McAllister, Gerald, TB, 1987-88; CB, 1989
McAlpin, Harry Keith, OT, 1975; OG, 1976-77-78
McCain, Robert, E-HB, 1944-(c); 1945-(c)
McCall, D. A., FB-QB, 1915-16
McCall, E. F., C-G-E, 1911-12-13-(c)
McCall, J. W., RT-RH, 1908-09-10-(c)
McCaulla, Michael E., trnr., 1976
McCay, Jim, FL, 1990
McClarty, W. H., G, 1918
McClure, Wayne L. (Mac), LB, 1965-66; DE, 1967
McClure, Worthy P., ST, 1968-69-70
McCool, Robert A., FB, 1952-53-54
McCraney, James, E, 1966

McCrary, Conrad, Jr., DB, 1979; LB, 1980
McDaniels, Bennie O., G-E-HB, 1918-19-20-21
McDonald, Quentin, DT, 1977-78-79-81
McDonald, W. Percy, FB, 1907; RE, 1909
McDonnell, Augustus H., LH, 1906
McDowell, James R., sub., 1898-99
McElroy, Brian, DB, 1984
McElroy, H. S., E, 1918
McFarland, Ben, sub-LE, 1898; 1900
McFerrin, Charles P., G, 1894
McGee, Buford, TB, 1979-80-81-82-83-(co-c)
McGraw, Robert (Bob), DT, 1977
McIntosh, James T., RG, 1899
McKaskel, Jerry D., HB, 1955
McKay, Henry Earl, G, 1954-55-56
McKay, Rush, LT, 1960-61
McKellar, Frank Monroe, S, 1970; 1972
McKellar, George, mgr., 1958
McKellar, Lane, mgr., 1965
McKey, Noel Keith, DE, 1971; LB, 1972
McKibbens, Thomas R., Jr., C, 1968
McKinney, Bob L., T-C, 1952-53-54
McKinney, David, QB, 1984-85-86
McKinney, Ronnie, RB, 1988-89
McKinzie, Ralph Wm. (Mackey), DE, 1972;
   DT, 1974
McLean, George D., HB, 1894-95-96-(c)
McLeish, Thomas, TE, 1990-91-92
McLeod, Larry Mikell, OT, 1974
McLeod, W. N., LG-C, 1905-06-07
McMillin, David, TE, 1982
McMurphy, Fred H., sub., 1899
McNeal, Theodis, DE, 1976-77-78
McPherren, Charles A., G, 1894-95
McQueen, Marvin Earl, Jr., E, 1964-65-66
McWilliams, Howard, T-G, 1934-35
McWright, Billy, HB, 1945

M

Mabry, Ed L., E, 1929
MacNeill, John B., C, 1973-74-75
Maddox, John Cullen, RE, 1963-64-65
Maddox, Milton Roland, trnr., 1959
Madre, John G., 1934-35-36
Magee, Robert M. (Mike), WG-SG, 1965-66-67
Magee, Wm. T. (Tommy), MM, 1969-70
Magruder, John M., QB-RH, 1901-02
Majure, Toby, HB, 1946
Malouf, Wm. A. (Bill), SE-QB, 1972-73; QB, 1974
Mangum, Ernest G. (Pete), FB, 1951-52-53
Mann, B. F., T, 1946-47
Mann, William, HB, 1937-38
Manning, Elisha Archie, III, QB, 1968-69-70-(co-c)
Manship, Doug J., FB, 1911
Markow, Gregory D., DE, 1972-73-74
Markow, Peter J., Jr., CB, 1972-73; SS, 1974
Marshall, Wm. D. (Bill), OG, 1973-74
Martin, Bobby, SE, 1986-87
Martin, Van, HB, 1924-25
Mask, James E., LE, 1950-51-52
Mason, James P., OT, 1972-73-74
Massengale, Kent, HB, 1937-38
Massengale, Marc B., C, 1978-79; OG, 1980
Massey, Charles Patrick, HB-mgr., 1949; 1951
Matthews, A. D., SS, 1986-87
Matthews, E. William, Jr., (Bill), WB, 1965-66-67
Matthews, James R., FB, 1952
Matthews, William L., sub., 1898
Mattina, Rodney A., LG, 1962-63-64
Maxwell, Harold L., LE, 1949-50-51
May, Arthur Wm. (Bill), DT, 1972-73
May, Christopher, OG, 1992
May, Doug, trnr., 1970
May, Jerry L., LG, 1951-52
Mayfield, Charles R., FB, 1917
Mays, Brian, NG, 1990-91-92
Meaders, E. L., LE, 1906
Meeks, Jessie L., trnr., 1975
Melton, James (Wesley), OT, 1990-91; OG-OT, 1992
Metz, John Stephen, FB, 1964
Mickles, Joe, FB, 1984-85-86-87-88
Mikul, Daniel P., OG, 1971-72-73
Miller, James G., P, 1976-77-78-79
Miller, Martin Van Buren, mgr., 1908
Miller, Michael T., SE, 1978
Miller, Vernon Terry, Jr., LB, 1973
Millette, T. J., HB, 1950
Mills, Ralph, T, 1913
Mills, Wilmer R., C, 1964
Milner, E. C., Jr., mgr., 1959
Milstead, Don M. (Mike), C, 1968
Mims, Crawford J., RG, 1951-52-53
Mims, Gerald C., G, 1978
Mims, Marvin Taylor, C, 1964
Mitchell, Adam H., Jr. (Buddy), WT, 1968-69-70
Mitchell, Chris, CB, 1987; DB, 1988; SS, 1989-90 (co-c)
Mitchell, John I., Jr., G, 1959; 1961
Mitchell, Lansing L., Jr., mgr., 1972
Mitchell, R. P., mgr., 1909
Mitchell, Russell B., OT, 1980-81-82

Mitchell, Steve F., HB, 1909-10-11-(c)
Moffett, Timothy, FLK, 1981; SE, 1982-83-84-(co-c)
Moley, Stanley Anthony, DHB, 1970-71-72
Moncus, Darrell, C, 1992
Monsour, Thomas Joseph, LB, 1970; DE, 1971
Montgomery, Alvin D., mgr., 1982
Montgomery, Charles L., LT, 1950-51-52
Montgomery, John, HB, 1920-21-22-23-(c)
Montgomery, Lavelle, E, 1931-32-33
Montgomery, Tyrone, WR, 1990-91
Moore, Hugh W., LT-C, 1907-08
Moore, Jeff, trainer, 1990-91
Moore, John, FL, 1989
Moore, Mark S., OT, 1979-80
Moore, Stevon, DB, 1985, CB, 1986-87-88 (co-c)
Moreland, Brian, LB, 1977-78-79
Morgan, Gerald, QB, 1957
Morgan, Keith, mgr., 1982
Morganti, Charles, LT, 1951-52
Morphis, Rex, T, 1928-29
Morris, Ben, DE, 1984-85-86
Morris, Charles A., TB, 1960-61-62
Morris, C. H. (Bill), G-T-E, 1927-28-29
Morris, Gregory, WR, 1992
Morris, Herman G., 1927
Morris, L. B., FB, 1918-19
Morrow, George C. (Buz), DT, 1967-68-69
Mosby, Herman Wm., SG, 1969-70
Moses, Ronald David, DE, 1970-71
Moses, Samuel S., Jr. (Rollo), RG, 1963-64
Moss, Charles E., Jr., FS, 1974; RCB, 1975-76
Moss, Edgar, C, 1903-04
Moss, Howard, DB, 1984; SS, 1985-86-87
Mounger, E. H., 1895
Muckle, Wayne, OG, 1989
Muirhead, Allen, RH, 1951-52-53-54-(co-c)
Muirhead, Jack, LB, 1989; OLB, 1990-91; DE, 1992
Mullins, Roy Lee "Chucky", FS, 1989
Mullins, Tim, trainer, 1988-89-90
Murff, Dan E., TB, 1973; DE, 1974-75
Murphey, Greg, mgr., 1990-91-92
Murphy, C. E., G, 1914
Murphy, Harvey A. (Ham), E, 1938-39
Murphy, Thomas, E, 1937
Murray, Hugh, mgr., 1962
Muse, Carl W., FLK, 1975
Mustin, John W., HB, 1923-24-25-(c)
Mustin, Robert Wm. (Billy), HB, 1946-47-48-49
Myers, Charles William, QB, 1964-65
Myers, Dale, G, 1941-42
Myers, L. D., G-T, 1911-12; 1914
Myers, Mark, trainer, 1986
Myers, Ricky, SE, 1985-86
Myers, Riley D., SE, 1968-69; 1971-(co-c)
Myers, William D., FB, 1899-(c); 1900-(c)

N

Nasif, George Milid, Jr., CB, 1974-75-76
Neely, Charles Wyck, WB-TB, 1968; DHB, 1969-70
Neely, Paul, FB, 1915-16
Nelson, Charles (Tex), C, 1933-34-35
Nelson, James Mitchell, LG-LB, 1963-64-65
Nesmith, Malcolm Dwayne, LB, 1981-82-83-(co-c)

Lawrence Johnson, defensive tackle

Newcomb, Mac, WR, 1984
Newell, Ronald Bruce, S, 1965; QB, 1966-67
Nichols, Rodney J., trnr., 1974
Niebuhr, Robert Bryan, OT, 1974; DLT, 1976; MG, 1977-78
Noblin, Jeff, DB, 1984; FS, 1985-86
Norman, Charles R. (Chuck), P, 1965-66
North, Roy, E, 1940
Northam, Larry Ray, DT, 1970; OT, 1971; TE, 1972
Nunn, Freddie Joe, DE, 1981-82-83-84-(co-c)

O

Odom, Jack L., E, 1947-48
Olander, Carl John (Bubba), OG, 1976-77
O'Malley, Sean, NG, 1991-92
O'Mara, B. B., C, 1918; 1921
Orr, Deano, OLB, 1990; LB, 1991; DE, 1992
Osgood, Chris, QB, 1985-86
Oswalt, Robert J., QB, 1946-47-48
Otis, James C., DE, 1979-80-81; LB, 1982
Ott, Dennis H., G-T, 1952-53
Ott, Reggie, FB-HB, 1951-52
Ott, Timothy A., DT, 1978
Owen, Bryan, K, 1985-86-87-88 (co-c)
Owen, Joe Sam, FB, 1969
Owen, Robert L., WG, 1968
Owen, Sam Walton, LG, 1961-62
Owens, Darrick, SE, 1990; WR, 1991
Owens, Robert L., T, 1957-58-59

P

Pace, W. Reginald (Reggie), C, 1974-75-76-(co-c)
Parham, David Howard, OG, 1971-72; OT, 1973
Parish, Randy, mgr., 1989-90-91
Parker, Edd Tate, E-T, 1951-52-53
Parker, Thomas, E-T, 1936-37-38
Parkes, James C., Jr., C, 1966-67-68
Parkes, Robert S., RCB, 1976
Parkes, Roger B., CB, 1973
Parks, Hugh Harold (Hank), SE, 1970
Parrott, Reggie, LB, 1987-88-89-90
Partin, Alan Wayne, OT, 1981-82
Paslay, Lea C., HB-QB, 1951-52-53; 1956
Patch, Dan, QB, 1944
Pate, Jeff, mgr., 1986
Pate, Joey, mgr., 1983-84
Patridge, C. K. (Dewey), FB-RH, 1957-58-59
Patterson, Jerome, T, 1915
Patton, Elack Chastine, HB, 1894
Patton, Houston, QB-HB, 1953-54-55
Patton, James R., Jr., HB, 1952-53-54-(co-c)
Patty, J. W., E, 1927-28-29
Payne, I. J., E, 1928-29-30
Peabody, Greg, K, 1987
Pearce, Rex, HB, 1944
Pearson, Thomas H. (Babe), LT, 1947-48-49-50
Peel, John, DE, 1977-78-79
Peeples, Everett U., E, 1928-29-30-(c)
Pegram, James Allen, TE, 1975
Pennington, Gerard M. (Jerry), RG, 1976
Perkins, A. P., G, 1923-24
Perkins, James B., Jr., RG-mgr., 1905-06
Perkins, P. A., sub, 1904
Perry, Leon, Jr., FB, 1976; TB, 1977-78; FB, 1979
Perry, Mario, TE, 1984-85-86
Perry, Monty, OG, 1989-90
Peters, Ned, HB, 1934-35-36
Pettey, Thomas J. (Joe), E, 1962-63-64
Pettis, William S., Jr., mgr., 1900
Pfeffer, W. L., FB, 1907
Phenix, Patrick J., OT, 1979-80-81-82
Phillips, Forrest C., Jr., mgr., 1979-80-81
Phillips, Hermon B., E, 1947
Philpot, Cory, RB, 1991-92 (co-c)
Pierce, Richard Wayne, C, 1982-83-84
Pierce, Tommy, mgr., 1983
Pigford, W. L., mgr., 1917
Pilkinton, S. T., T-G-E, 1905-06; 1911
Pittman, James Bradley (Brad), CB, 1974; SS, 1975-76
Pittman, Thomas Michael (Mike), DT, 1974-75-76
Pitts, Quintin, TB, 1984
Pivarnik, John, T, 1940
Plasketes, George M., QB-DE, 1975; DLE, 1976-(co-c); DE, 1977-(co-c)
Poole, Calvin Phillip, G, 1946-47-48
Poole, George Barney, LE, 1942; 1947-48
Poole, Jack Lewyl, E, 1948-49
Poole, James E. (Buster), LE, 1934-35-36
Poole, James E., Jr., TE, 1969-70-71
Poole, Oliver L., T, 1946
Poole, Ray S., RE, 1941-42; 1946 (c)
Poole, Ray S., Jr., TE, 1976
Pope, Carl Allen, TB, 1965
Popp, Romeo, FB-QB, 1939-40
Porter, James Edward, FB, 1970-71-72
Porter, Frank, FB, 1983; DB, 1984; SS, 1985
Portis, Michael, DE, 1982; NG, 1983-84-85-(co-c)

Head Coach Ken Cooper (1974-77)

Posey, H. H., 1895
Potts, Ed, G, 1930
Powe, Alexander, M., QB, 1908
Powell, Eric, FS, 1986
Powell, Kelly Newton, QB, 1981-82-83 (co-c)
Powell, Kenneth W., RG, 1960
Powell, Travis, mgr., 1962
Powers, Jimmy T., 1954
Prater, Charles, OLB, 1988
Price, Charles, E, 1930
Price, Don, CB, 1986-87-88-89
Price, James Richard, LG, 1958-59-60
Price, Jarratt, FB, 1978-79
Priestly, Harry D., Jr., 1897-(c)
Prince, T. J., G, 1925-24
Pritchett, Kelvin, NG, 1988-89-90 (co-c)
Pruett, Billy Riddell, C-G, 1955-56-57
Pruett, Dawson, C, 1987-88-89-90 (co-c)
Puryear, H. H., G, 1911-12

R

Radford, Jimmy W., mgr., 1973
Ranatza, Michael A., C, 1974
Randall, George M. (Buck), FB, 1961-62-63
Randolph, Vivian, QB, 1911
Ratcliff, Culley C., HB, 1920
Rather, Edward, mgr., 1939
Ray, E. H., C-HB-T, 1917-18 (c); 1919
Ray, Joe, FB, 1982
Ray, S. T., FB, 1930
Rayborn, Jerry Joe, E, 1963
Rayburn, Tony, OG, 1984; OG-C, 1985-(co-c)
Redhead, John A., Jr., sub., RT, 1898-99-1900
Reed, Benton, DT, 1983-84-85
Reed, Edwin, WR, 1990
Reed, Garland R. (Randy), TB, 1969; TB-FB, 1970; TB, 1971
Reed, James M., TB, 1973-74-75
Reed, John B. (Jack), QB-S, 1951-52
Reed, John E., mgr., 1907
Reed, S. Leroy, Jr., LH, 1955-56-57
Reeder, Herbert E., 1931
Regan, George Bernie, E, 1959
Reid, Ed, RT, 1924; QB, 1925
Reiley, Marion W., RT, 1903
Renshaw, Paul, sub., RE-QB, 1906; 1908-09
Reynolds, Robert R., E, 1916
Rhodes, Jeff, OG, 1986; OT, 1987-88; OG, 1989
Rice, Tommy, mgr., 1963
Richards, Tyrone, FB, 1976-77-78
Richardson, Jerry Dean, LE, 1965-66-67
Richardson, John A., FB, 1964-65

Richardson, Marion L., Jr., (Mel), LB-DE, 1972-73
Richardson, Ricky, DE, 1986-87; OLB, 1988-89
Richardson, William, T, 1933-34-35
Richmond, W. M., 1895
Richter, Todd, FS, 1985
Ricks, W. B., mgr., 1898
Riddell, T. H., C-HB, 1919-20
Roane, Ralph H., LT, 1900
Robbins, Michael D. (Mike), TB, 1966-67
Roberson, J. Lake, JR., RG, 1938-39-40
Roberson, Shed H., E, 1932-33-34
Roberson, Shed H., Jr., RG, 1958-59
Roberts, Bobby David, SE, 1969
Roberts, Camp, FL, 1988; TE, 1989-90
Roberts, Fred F., Jr., FB, 1961-62-63
Roberts, George, G, 1942
Roberts, James B., T, 1960-61-62
Roberts, Kelly, RE, 1965
Roberts, Pinky, G, 1914
Robertson, Daniel D., LB, 1979-80-81-82
Robertson, G. H., sub.-RG, 1905-06
Robertson, Jeff, mgr., 1984
Robertson, Joseph E., LT, 1958-59-60
Robertson, Randy, trnr., 1983-84
Robertson, Reginald M., FB, 1960
Robertson, Steven B. (Chip), mgr., 1976
Robertson, Will E. (Pete), DT, 1973-74-75; MG, 1976
Robinson, Bobby Dewitt, LG, 1962-63-64-(co-c)
Robinson, George O., sub.-c., 1899
Robinson, Howard D., FB, 1919-20-21-(c)
Robinson, John W., FB-RH, 1958-59-60
Robinson, Michael, CB, 1988-89-90
Robinson, William Robert, KS, 1981
Rodgers, Andree, FL, 1983-84-85
Rodgers, Paul C., FB, 1950
Rodgers, Rab, HB, 1933-34-35
Rogers, Daniel B., mgr., 1974
Rose, Henry, FB, 1944
Ross, John, mgr., 1990-91-92
Ross, John R., WR, 1992
Ross, L. A., FB-QB, 1929-30-31
Ross, Lynn, LB, 1991-92 (co-c)
Ross, Richard D., C, 1960-61-62
Ross, Warner A. (Nubbin), C, 1983-84-85
Roudebush, A. H., LE, 1893-(c)
Rounsaville, C. L., E, 1932-33-34
Rowan, Leon F., G, 1917
Ruby, Pete, C-QB, 1931-32-33
Rucker, Robert R. (Randy), SS, 1976
Rushing, Herbert (Doodle), HB, 1928
Russell, Jack, G, 1945
Russell, Lucius Thompson, LG, 1893
Russell, Michael W. (Coot), C, 1978-79-80
Russell, Richard H. (Stump), LB, 1972-73-74-(tri-c)
Rutledge, L. J., LG, 1904

S

Salley, David W., HB, 1950
Salley, James W., HB, 1950
Salloum, Mitchell, T, 1923; 1925-26
Salmon, Farley, RH, 1945-46-47; QB, 1948
Sam, Billy, RH, 1939-40-41
Samuels, E. S., G, 1912
Sanders, Aubrey E., RT, 1957-58
Sanders, Donald Wayne, mgr., 1970
Sanders, Wm. Ervin, T, 1938
Sanders, William H., mgr., 1951
Sandroni, Todd, FS, 1987-88-89-90
Sartin, Daniel M. (Dan), LT, 1965-66-67-(co-c)
Sarver, Jeff, SE, 1988
Saul, James K., SE, 1965-66
Savage, James, DE, 1984
Scales, Ewell D., LH, 1893; T, 1894-95-(c)
Schimmel, Jay, OT, 1985-86-87
Schneller, Bill, QB, 1937-38-39-(c)
Scott, Arthur, DE, 1985-86-87; OLB, 1988
Scruggs, Arthur, E, 1921-22
Searfoss, Stephen A., OG, 1978; 1980-81-82
Sears, Billy, FB, 1945
Seawright, Norman H., SE, 1978-79
Seay, Clant J. M., mgr., 1934
Seymour, Arnold, NG, 1982-83
Shands, Harley R., sub., 1898
Sharman, J. R., T-E, 1915-16
Sharp, L. V., E, 1951
Sharpe, Elmer C., LT-sub., 1898; 1900
Shaw, Guy Andrew, MG, 1979-80; C, 1981; OT, 1982
Shaw, Maurice, RB, 1989-90
Shaw, Vernon, T, 1935
Sheehan, Eric, OT, 1983-84-85
Sheffield, Don W., mgr., 1961
Shelby, John, QB, HB, 1942; 1948
Shelley, Jonathan, CB, 1983-84-85-86
Shepherd, Archie, C-G, 1952-53-54
Shields, Frank L., LH-RH, 1910-11
Shields, John R., LH-FB, 1905; 1909
Shinault, James Rushing, E, 1894
Shoemaker, Allen C., HB, 1932-33-34

All-America tackle Rex Reed Boggan (bottom) holds up a stack of linemen: Boggan, James Waters, Billy Sullivan, Bob Adams, Dave Dickerson, Gene Dubuisson, Buddy Alliston

Wesley Walls, All-America end

Shoemaker, James, G, 1915
Shows, Henry N. (Hank), TE, 1966-67-68 (co-c)
Shows, James Larry, RT, 1964-65-66
Shows, Russ, QB, 1989-90-91-92 (co-c)
Shumaker, Leo, RE, 1904
Shumaker, Michael E. (Mike), TE, 1968
Simmons, Clyde D. (Doug), Jr., HB, 1969
Simmons, Delmar, 1924
Simmons, James, TE, 1986-87
Simmons, L. G., E, 1917-18
Simmons, Wm. M. (Bill), TE, 1972
Simpson, Glynne, mgr., 1959
Simpson, Jack M., LG, 1955-56-57 (co-c)
Simpson, Jack R, DT, 1972
Singletary, Shannon, trainer, 1992
Sinquefield, Melvin H., C, 1950-51
Sisler, W. H., FB, 1917
Slay, James, LE, 1950-51-52
Sledge, James William, mgr., 1980
Small, Eddie, DB, 1990; WR, 1991-92
Small, Wm. N. (Bill), FLK, 1973; SE, 1974-75
Smith, B. A., HB, 1914
Smith, Ben P., E, 1893-94
Smith, Claude M. (Tad), HB, 1926-27-28
Smith, Darryl, NG, 1986-87-88-89
Smith, E. J. (Rudolph), LT, 1956-57-58
Smith, Eric L., DE, 1977-78-79
Smith, H. A., E, 1942; 1946
Smith, Howard E. (Bert), SE, 1976
Smith, James, TE, 1986-87
Smith, Kenneth O., T-G, 1963-64-65
Smith, L. A., RG, 1899
Smith, L. Q., FB, 1974; 1976; TE, 1977
Smith, Lee Joseph, G, 1940
Smith, Mac, K, 1988-89-90
Smith, Mark, RB-CB, 1992
Smith, Marley, T, 1932
Smith, Marvin G. (Erm), HB, 1938-39
Smith, Michael A., DB, 1980-81
Smith, Michael C., TE, 1982-83-84-85
Smith, O. R., T, 1922; 1924
Smith, Ralph A., LE, 1959-60-61-(t-c)
Smith, Ralph Guy, 1963
Smith, Richard Joel (Dicky), LB, 1970
Smith, Robert (Thunder), FB, 1984-85; LB, 1986-87
Smith, Robert T., TE, 1973
Smith, Steven H., LB, 1973-74
Smith, Stewart, E, 1940
Smith, Thomas Larry, HB, 1961-62-63
Smith, Timothy, OG, 1971-72
Smith, V. K., G, 1925-26-27
Smith, Wayne B., C, 1921-22-23-24
Smith, William (Bill), P/K, 1983-84-85-86
Smithson, Claude T., HB, 1921-22-23-24-(c)
Smylie, J. B., 1895

Smythe, Frank W., LE, 1913-14-(c)
Snyder, Michael E., trnr., 1974-75
Soehn, Woody, OT, 1984, 1986, 1987; C, 1985
Somerville, Robert, Jr., 1903-04-05
Southerland, Trea, FS, 1989; SS, 1990; CB, 1991; SS, 1992
Sowder, Shawn, TE, 1987-88
Sparks, Michael, OT, 1990-91
Spears, James W., RG, 1958
Spiers, Tommy, QB, 1952
Spivey, R. E., E, 1920
Spore, Jerry P., SAF, 1978
Stagg, Leonard, HB, 1942
Stallings, Danny Lee, DHB, 1970-71; SE, 1973
Stearns, Michael P., OT, 1980-81
Steele, Wm. Scott, LB, 1972-73-74; DE, 1975
Stennis, Dudley, T, 1894
Stephens, Hubert D., G, 1894; E, 1895
Stephens, Rogers, K, 1991-92
Stevens, P. J., PK, 1982
Stevens, W. R. B., mgr., 1913
Stewart, H. F. (Chip), WT, 1966; TE, 1967
Stewart, James, DE, 1984
Stewart, Jerry, LB, 1982-83
Stewart, Joel, CB, 1977-78-79-80 (co-c)
Stigler, Samuel James, mgr., 1958
Still, Claude, sub., 1893
Stolt, John J., LG, 1955
Stone, Ed G., QB, 1931-32-33
Stone, Henry Jerry, C, 1954-55-56
Storey, James W., LB, 1974; FB, 1975-76-77
Stovall, John A., G-T, 1922-23
Straughn, Robert, G, 1951
Street, Donald Earl, FB, 1965-66-67
Stribling, James A. (Jack), LE, 1946-47-48-49
Stribling, Majure B. (Bill), RE, 1945; 1948-49-50
Strickland, Randolph T., C, 1905
Stringer, L. O., QB, 1923
Strother, Adrian, OT, 1989-90
Stroud, Damon, mgr., 1986, 1988, 1989
Stuart, George E., LB, 1974-75-76 (co-c)
Stuart, James B., III, DE, 1971; DT, 1972; LB, 1973-(co-c)
Stuart, J. Graham, DB, 1979-80
Stubblefield, Jerry, QB, 1965
Studdard, Vernon, WB, 1968-70
Sullivan, Charles J., SE, 1966-67
Sullivan, Frank, FS, 1991-92
Sullivan, John, mgr., 1963
Sullivan, Louie Wesley, RE, 1960-61-62
Sultan, Dan I., LT, 1902
Sumners, Chester L., T, 1917
Sumrall, Wm. W., TB, 1962-64

Sutherland, Leslie S., FS, 1973; SS, 1974
Sutton, Steve, C, 1986-87
Swatzell, Scott, RB, 1989-90-91
Swayze, Tom K., E, 1930-31-32
Sweet, Michael W., TB-SE, 1974; TB, 1975-76
Swetland, Michael R. (Mike), WG, 1965-66-67
Swinney, C. P., C, 1940-41
Swor, Zollie Alton, E, 1931-32
Sykes, Shawn, TB, 1985-86-87-88

T

Taylor, Charles (Chico), LH, 1960-61
Taylor, Harry, E, 1948
Taylor, J. Lee, mgr., 1979-80-81-82
Taylor, Leslie Edward, Jr., G, 1965-66-67
Taylor, Tommy F., RH, 1956-57-58
Teevan, Neil, K, 1983
Tempfer, J. G. (Chuck), LE, 1961
Templeton, Billy, LE, 1956-57-58
Terracin, Steve Wayne, E, 1964-65-66
Terrell, Marvin, Jr., G, 1957-58-59
Terrell, James M. (Mitch), TB, 1962
Terrell, Ray, RH, 1941
Terry, Decker L., C-G, 1957-58
Thames, Mickey, OG, 1977-78-79
Thaxton, James Cairy, RG, 1964
Therrel, J. S., E, 1912
Thigpen, Ed, FB, 1987; RB, 1989-90
Thomas, Andre, RB, 1980-81; FB, 1982
Thomas, Dalton (Pepper), LH, 1954
Thomas, Darryl, CB, 1983
Thomas, James Larry, LB, 1968; MG, 1969
Thomas, Jim Earl, RB, 1987; TB, 1988; RB, 1989-90
Thomas, Lemay, WR, 1992
Thomas, Marquise, OLB, 1991; DE, 1992
Thomas, Roville (Bobo), DB, 1980
Thompson, Keith, DE, 1987; OLB, 1988-89
Thompson, Robert, G, 1925
Thompson, Robert P., RH, 1898
Thompson, Robert W., G, 1919
Thompson, Steve, trainer, 1990
Thornton, Chester, TB, 1979
Thornton, James Ray, E, 1951
Thornton, Johnny H., DT, 1978
Thornton, Nathan, RB, 1991-92
Thorsey, Frank, E, 1940-41-42
Tiblier, Jerome J., FB-RH, 1944; 1947-48
Tillery, Douglas W., FB, 1962
Tillman, James S., FB, 1938-39-40
Tillman, Ronald, TB, 1965
Timmons, Aaron, HB, 1944
Tipton, Julius R., RE, 1893-94
Toler, Kenneth P., SE, 1978-79-80 (co-c)
Torgerson, Larry Donald, OG, 1968; DT, 1969-70
Totten, G. C., 1924
Townes, Clarence Henry, HB, 1894
Townes, Jack A., mgr., 1964
Townsend, Andre, DT, 1981-82-83 (co-c)
Transou, Lewis, mgr., 1940
Trapp, Franklin Wm., LB, 1966-67-68
Trapp, Lee H., G, 1930-31-32-(c)
Trauth, Marvin H., LT, 1950-51-52
Travis, Brent, mgr., 1989-90
Traxler, David, OG, 1977-78-79
Trimble, William, G, 1933
Trotter, William C., LH-LE, 1907-08-09-(c); 1910
Truett, George W., E, 1952
Truitt, Eric, DB, 1982-83-84; CB, 1985
Tuggle, Jimmy, FB, 1952
Turnbow, Guy, T-FB, 1930-31-32
Turner, Chris, TE, 1991-92
Turner, Gary W., DE, 1973-74-75-76
Turner, John H., Jr., LG, 1964
Turner, Thomas N., G, 1929
Tyler, Breck, FLK, 1980-81

U

Upchurch, Robert K., C, 1961-62-63
Urbanek, James E., RT, 1965-67
Uzzle, Robert H., DE, 1966-68

V

Vacca, Richard W., DE, 1979
Valverde, Charles V., LG-LE, 1907-08
VanDevender, Wm. J. (Billy), MM, 1968-69-70
Vandevere, Wm. E., E, 1911-12
Vann, Clay, OLB, 1990; DE, 1992
Vann, Thad (Pie), T, 1926-27-28-(c)
Vaughan, Robert C., DT-WT, 1965-66-67
Vaughn, Gerald, CB, 1989; SS, 1991; FS, 1992
Veasley, Jeremy, FB, 1992
Veazey, Burney, S, TE, 1971-72-73
Vega, Chad, mgr., 1990-91-92

W

Wade, Robert Myers (Bobby), FB, 1965-66-67
Wainwright, Ralph, C, 1899

Wakefield, Victor Reed, Jr., LCB, 1973; TB, 1974
Walker, Donald, trainer, 1977-78
Walker, Gerald H., HB, 1928
Walker, Gregory Scott, TE, 1981-82; TE-OT, 1983; OT, 1984
Walker, Harrison Carroll, Jr., QB, 1965-66
Walker, Harvey W., QB, 1926-27-28
Walker, Paul L., mgr., 1973
Walker, Richard H., G, 1922-23
Walker, Terrence C., OG, 1975; OT, 1976-77-79
Wallis, James H. (Jimmy), QB, 1967-68; MM, 1969
Walls, Wesley, DE, 1985-86-87; TE-DE, 1988 (co-c)
Walsh, Willie Henry, MM, 1970; SS, 1971; RCB, 1972
Walters, James A., T, 1953-54
Walton, Byron S., RE, 1910-11
Wamble, James E., LB, 1976
Wander, Mose, mgr., 1933
Ward, Harry, mgr., 1926
Ward, Jesse Davis, LE, 1937-38
Ware, Cassius, LB, 1992
Warfield, Gerald Wayne, MM, 1964-65; S, 1966
Warner, Jack, QB, 1945
Warren, Homer E., HB, 1916
Watkins, Dennis R., RT, 1976; OG, 1978
Watkins, Thomas B., QB, 1900-01; 1903
Watson, Bill E., G-T, 1949-50-51
Watson, Henry D., Jr., RE, 1907
Watson, R. Virgil, G-T, 1914; 1916
Watson, Thomas C., QB, 1904
Weatherly, James D., QB, 1962-63-64
Weathers, Curtis L., TE, 1974; 1976-77-78 (c)
Webb, Hunter, G, 1942
Webb, Jay, DE, 1984-85-(co-c)
Webb, Luther Wade, FB, 1970; DT, 1971
Webb, Reed S., WG, 1966-67
Webster, Edgar, sub., LE, 1903-04-05
Weese, Norris Lee, QB, 1971-72-73-(co-c)
Weiss, Richard T., 1952-53-54-55

Billy Ray Adams, All-America fullback

Weiss, Richard, Jr., OG, 1978
Wells, David Kent, WB, 1963-64-65
Wells, Vernon, QB, 1945
West, Carl E., FB, 1950-51
West, John Wayne, LT, 1955-56-57
Westerman, Richard W., HB, 1950-51-52
Westmoreland, Daniel, TE, 1989-90
Wettlin, D. G., QB, 1906
Whitaker, David, T, 1942
Whitaker, Murray P., OT, 1976-77-78
White, Abner, C, 1990-91
White, Brad, FB-HB, 1931-32-33
White, Brad, CB, 1978-79-80
White, Hugh L., C-LG, 1898-99-1900
White, James Thomas, FB, 1960
White, John U., Jr., OG, 1974
White, Lloyd, G, 1936-37
White, Robert P. (Randy), OG-C, 1975; C, 1976; OG, 1977
Whitener, Larry J., G, 1966-67
Whiteside, Lance, CB, 1991-92
Whiteside, Paul L., HB, 1951
Whitten, L. D., E, 1917
Whittington, John, HB, 1938
Whittington, O. M., 1921
Wigley, Daniel, DT, 1986-87-88-89
Wilburn, Barry Todd, DB, 1981-82-83-84

Wilcox, Reuben D., HB, 1927-28-29
Wilford, Dan S., E, 1961
Wilford, Ned B., E, 1961
Wilkins, Ernest, RG, 1905
Wilkins, Joseph T., III, LE, 1962-64
Williams, B. Frank, QB, 1907
Williams, Bill, T, 1937
Williams, D. E., 1895
Williams, David Wayne, G, 1981
Williams, Don N., RE, 1955-56-57
Williams, Freddie Lee, TB, 1976-77-78; WR, 1979
Williams, G. H., G, 1920
Williams, Gary Neil, LB, 1971; DE, 1972
Williams, J. M., 1921
Williams, John, trnr., 1983-84
Williams, John C., Jr., G, 1954-55
Williams, Ken, OL, 1988; OG, 1989
Williams, Murray L., Jr., ST, 1968
Williams, Nakita, LB, 1979-80-81-82
Williams, Robert J. (Ben), DT, 1972-73-74; DT-MG, 1975-(tri-c)
Williams, Robert W., DB, 1980
Williams, Sebastian "Snake", OLB, 1989; DT, 1990-91; OT-DT, 1992
Williamson, John D. (Hotshot), T, 1926
Williamson, Terry, NG, 1982-83-84
Wilson, Charles (Buddy), C-E, 1933-34
Wilson, David, G, 1934-35-36
Wilson, Robert, HB, 1946-47-48-49
Wilson, Stacy, DL, 1991; DE, 1992
Windham, Donald W., RG, 1962-63-64
Windham, John, E, 1925-26
Winstead, Bobby Ray, SG, 1968
Winstead, Jimmy LeRoy, TB, 1971; FB, 1972; TE, 1974
Winston, Lowell, T, 1957
Winter, Michael Todd, trainer, 1988-89-90-91
Winther, Richard L. (Wimpy), C, 1969-70
Wise, Billy, TE, 1978-79-80
Wisozki, Ray, T, 1941
Wohlgemuth, John T., TE, 1970; OT, '71
Wonsley, Nathan, TB, 1983-84-85-(co-c)
Wood, Andrew, RE, 1906-07-(c)
Wood, Charles G., C, 1971-73
Wood, Dan, C, 1941-42-(c)
Wood, Meredith, HB, 1930
Woodruff, James Lee (Cowboy), HB, 1957-58-59
Woodruff, Lee T. (Cowboy), FB, 1927-28-29
Woods, Joe, WR, 1992
Woodward, H. G., QB, 1923
Woodward, Ray, HB, 1942
Worley, Michael, SS, 1992
Worsham, Jerry Dean, G, 1963
Woullard, Reginald, SE, 1975; TB, 1976-78-79
Wrenn, R. B., C, 1914-15
Wylie, Phillip, LB, 1978-79-80

Y

Yandell, Robert, HB, 1941-42
Yarbo, Welborn, T, 1916
Yelverton, Billy G., E-T, 1952; 1954-55-56
Yerger, J. S., FB, 1903
Yerger, Wm. G., sub., 1903
Young, Carl R., G, 1949-50
Young, John Wm., Jr. (Bill), SE, 1970-71
Young, Mark, QB, 1985-86-87-88

Z

Zanone, Curtis, J., mgr., 1974
Zeppelin, Deron, TE, 1987; OL, 1988
Zullo, Michael, mgr., 1985-86

Bill Smith, All-America punter

Buford McGee, tailback

Yearly Results

Since 1893

All-Time Football Scores

1893 – Won 4, Lost 1

		OM	Opp.
Nov. 11	SWBU,* Oxford	56	0
Nov. 18	Memphis A. C., Memphis	16	0
Nov. 25	SWBU, Jackson, Tenn.	36	0
Nov. 30	So. A. C., New Orleans	0	24
Dec. 2	Tulane, New Orleans	12	4
	TOTAL POINTS:	120	28

COACH: Dr. A. L. Bondurant.
CAPTAIN: Alfred H. Roudebush, LE.

Known from 1908 as Union University.

1894 – Won 6, Lost 1

Oct. 20	St. Thomas Hall, Oxford	62	0
Oct. 27	Alabama, Jackson	6	0
Nov. 10	Vanderbilt, Nashville	0	40
Nov. 12	*Cumberland, Lebanon	—	—
Nov. 17	Memphis A. C., Memphis	12	0
Nov. 29	Tulane, New Orleans	8	2
Dec. 1	So. A. C., New Orleans	†6	0
Dec. 3	LSU, Baton Rouge	26	6
	TOTAL POINTS:	120	48

COACH: C. D. Clark.
CAPTAIN: Wm. Henry Cook, FB.

Game cancelled.   †Forfeit.

1895 – Won 2, Lost 1

Oct. 12	St. Thomas Hall, Oxford	18	0
Nov. 23	Memphis A. C., Memphis	2	0
	Tulane, New Orleans	4	28
Dec. 9	*LSU, Oxford	—	—
	TOTAL POINTS:	24	28

COACH: H. L. Fairbanks.
CAPTAIN: Ewell D. Scales, LHB.

Game cancelled.

1896 – Won 1, Lost 2

	St. Thomas Hall, Oxford	20	0
Nov. 13	LSU, Vicksburg	4	12
Nov. 26	Tulane, New Orleans	0	10
	TOTAL POINTS:	24	22

COACH: J. W. Hollister.
CAPTAIN: George D. McLean.

1897

No Team Due to Yellow Fever Epidemic.
COACH: None.
CAPTAIN: Harry D. Priestly.

1898 – Won 1, Lost 1

Dec. 12	Tulane, New Orleans	9	14
Dec. 17	St. Thomas Hall, Oxford	9	2
	TOTAL POINTS:	18	16

COACH: T. G. Scarbrough.
CAPTAIN: Eugene Campbell, RG.

1899 – Won 3, Lost 4

Oct. 27	*Central U., Memphis	13	6
Oct. 28	U. of Nashville, Oxford	0	11
Nov. 1	LSU, Meridian	11	0
Nov. 4	Vanderbilt, Memphis	0	11
Nov. 12	Sewanee, Memphis	0	12
Nov. 24	Alabama, Jackson	5	7
Nov. 30	Tulane, New Orleans	15	0
	TOTAL POINTS:	44	47

COACH: W. H. Lyon.
CAPTAIN: Wm. D. Myers, FB.

Merged with Centre College in 1901.

1963 SEC Champions

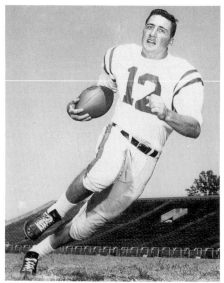

Jake Gibbs, All-America quarterback

1900 — Won 0, Lost 3

Oct. 6	Vanderbilt, Nashville	0	6
Oct. 26	Alabama, Tuscaloosa	5	12
Nov. 29	Tulane, New Orleans	0	12
	TOTAL POINTS:	5	30

COACH: Z. N. Estes, Jr.
CAPTAIN: Wm. D. Myers, FB.

1901 — Won 2, Lost 4

Oct. 12	*CBC, Oxford	—	—
Oct. 19	Mem. U. School, Oxford	6	0
Oct. 26	Alabama, Tuscaloosa	0	41
Oct. 28	†Miss. A&M, Starkville	0	17
Nov. 2	SWBU, Oxford	17	0
Nov. 8	LSU, Baton Rouge	0	46
Nov. 28	Tulane, New Orleans	11	25
	TOTAL POINTS:	34	129

COACHES: William Sibley; Daniel S. Martin.
CAPTAIN: F. W. Elmer, RE.

*Game cancelled.
†Known from 1932 as Mississippi State.

1902 — Won 4, Lost 3

Oct. 11	Vanderbilt, Nashville	0	29
Oct. 18	Cumberland, Oxford	38	0
Oct. 25	Miss. A&M, Starkville	21	0
Nov. 1	Mem. U. School, Oxford	42	0
Nov. 8	LSU, New Orleans	0	6
Nov. 15	Tennessee, Memphis	10	11
Nov. 27	Tulane, New Orleans	10	0
	TOTAL POINTS:	121	46

COACH: D. S. Martin.
CAPTAIN: John M. Foster, RHB.

1903 — Won 2, Lost 1, Tied 1

Oct. 24	Vanderbilt, Nashville	0	33
Nov. 7	*Mem. Med. Col., Memphis	17	0
Nov. 14	Miss. A&M, Oxford	6	6
Nov. 21	LSU, New Orleans	11	0
	TOTAL POINTS:	34	39

COACH: Mike Harvey.
CAPTAIN: F. W. Elmer, RHB.

*The Memphis Medical Hospital College until January, 1913, when it became the University of Tennessee School of Medicine.

1904 — Won 4, Lost 3

Oct. 15	Vanderbilt, Nashville	0	69
Oct. 22	Miss. A&M, Columbus	17	5
Oct. 29	SWBU, Oxford	114	0
Nov. 5	LSU, Baton Rouge	0	5
Nov. 12	Mem. Med. Col., Jackson	42	0
Nov. 19	*U. of Nashville, Memphis	12	5
Nov. 24	Tulane, New Orleans	0	22
	TOTAL POINTS:	185	106

COACH: Mike Harvey.
CAPTAIN: Allen P. Dodd, LT.

*Now George Peabody College, a part of Vanderbilt University.

1905 — Won 0, Lost 2

Nov. 20	Cumberland, Oxford	0	18
Nov. 30	Miss. A&M, Jackson	0	11
	TOTAL POINTS:	0	29

COACH: None.
CAPTAIN: Allen P. Todd, LT.

1906 — Won 4, Lost 2

Oct. 4	Maryville, Oxford	16	6
Oct. 13	Vanderbilt, Nashville	0	29
Oct. 20	LSU, Baton Rouge	9	0
Oct. 27	*Tennessee, Memphis	—	—
Nov. 3	Tulane, New Orleans	17	0
Nov. 12	Sewanee, Memphis	0	24
Nov. 17	*Arkansas, Little Rock	—	—
Nov. 29	Miss. A&M, Jackson	29	5
	TOTAL POINTS:	71	64

COACH: Tom S. Hammond.
CAPTAIN: Cleveland P. Huggins, FB.

*Game cancelled.

1907 — Won 0, Lost 6

Oct. 2	*SWBU, Oxford	—	—
Oct. 12	Alabama, Columbus	0	20
Oct. 19	Missouri Normal, Oxford	6	12
Oct. 26	Sewanee, Memphis	0	65
Nov. 9	Vanderbilt, Memphis	0	60
Nov. 16	LSU, Jackson	0	23
Nov. 28	Miss. A&M, Jackson	0	15
	TOTAL POINTS:	6	195

COACH: Frank Mason.
CAPTAIN: Andrew Wood, RE.

*Game cancelled.

1908 — Won 3, Lost 5

Oct. 3	Mem. U. School, Oxford	30	0
Oct. 10	Arkansas, Fayetteville	0	33
Oct. 17	Missouri Normal, Memphis	17	0
Oct. 24	Vanderbilt, Nashville	0	29
Oct. 29	Miss. College, Jackson	41	0
Oct. 31	Tulane, New Orleans	0	10
Nov. 10	*SPU, Oxford	5	9
Nov. 26	Miss. A&M, Jackson	6	44
	TOTAL POINTS:	99	125

COACH: Frank Kyle.
CAPTAIN: Ike C. Knox, RHB.

*Known as Southwestern (Memphis) from 1925.

1909 — Won 4, Lost 3, Tied 2

Oct. 2	Mem U. School, Oxford	18	0
Oct. 5	Mem. Med. Col., Oxford	15	0
Oct. 9	LSU, Baton Rouge	0	10
Oct. 16	Tulane, New Orleans	0	5
Oct. 23	Alabama, Jackson	0	0
Oct. 30	Vanderbilt, Nashville	0	17
Nov. 13	Henderson-Brown, Arkadelphia, Ark.	12	12
Nov. 18	Union, Oxford	45	0
Nov. 25	Miss. A&M, Jackson	9	5
	TOTAL POINTS:	99	49

COACH: Dr. Nathan P. Stauffer.
CAPTAIN: W. C. Trotter, LHB.

1910 — Won 7, Lost 1

Oct. 1	Memphis H. S., Oxford	10	0
Oct. 5	Mem. Med. Col., Oxford	2	0
Oct. 13	Tulane, New Orleans	16	0
Oct. 21	Miss. College, Clinton	24	0
Oct. 29	Vanderbilt, Nashville	2	9
Nov. 5	Alabama, Greenville	16	0
Nov. 12	Mem. Med. Col., Memphis	44	0
Nov. 24	Miss. A&M, Jackson	30	0
	TOTAL POINTS:	144	9

COACH: Dr. Nathan P. Stauffer.
CAPTAIN: John W. McCall, RHB.

1911 — Won 6, Lost 3

Sept. 30	†Memphis H.S., Oxford	42	0
Oct. 5	SPU, Oxford	41	0
Oct. 13	*Louisiana I. I., Oxford	15	0
Oct. 24	Henderson-Brown, Arkadelphia, Ark.	24	11
Oct. 27	Texas A&M, College Station	0	17
Oct. 30	Miss. College, Jackson	28	0
Nov. 4	Mercer, Macon, Ga.	34	0
Nov. 18	Vanderbilt, Nashville	0	21
Nov. 30	Miss. A&M, Jackson	0	6
	TOTAL POINTS:	184	55

COACH: Dr. Nathan P. Stauffer.
CAPTAIN: Steve F. Mitchell, LHB.

†First September Date.
*Known now as Louisiana Tech.

1912 — Won 5, Lost 3

Oct. 5	*Memphis H.S., Oxford	34	0
Oct. 12	Castle Heights, Oxford	†1	0
Oct. 19	LSU, Baton Rouge	10	7
Oct. 26	Vanderbilt, Nashville	0	24
Nov. 1	Miss. College, Oxford	12	0
Nov. 9	Alabama, Tuscaloosa	9	10
Nov. 13	Texas, Austin	14	53
Nov. 16	Mem. Med. Col., Memphis	47	6
	TOTAL POINTS:	127	100

COACH: Leo DeTray.
CAPTAIN: J. C. (Red) Adams, C.

†Forfeit. *Known from 1913 as Central High School.

1913 — Won 6, Lost 3, Tied 1

Oct. 8	VMI, Lexington, Va.	0	14
Oct. 11	VPI, Blacksburg, Va.	14	35
Oct. 15	Virginia Meds., Richmond	7	6
Oct. 23	Union, Oxford	46	0
Nov. 1	Louisiana I. I., Oxford	26	0
Nov. 7	Hendrix, Conway, Ark.	6	8
Nov. 15	Arkansas, Little Rock	21	10
Nov. 22	Cumberland, Memphis	7	0
Nov. 27	*Ms. Normal, Hattiesburg	13	7
Nov. 27	†Ouachita, Arkadelphia	0	0
	TOTAL POINTS:	140	80

COACH: William Driver.
CAPTAIN: E. Forrest McCall, E.

*Known now as Southern Mississippi.
†Correct Dates.

150

1914—Won 5, Lost 4, Tied 1

Oct. 3	†Arkansas Aggies, Oxford	20	0
Oct. 10	SPU, Oxford	14	0
Oct. 17	LSU, Baton Rouge	21	0
Oct. 28	Miss. College, Jackson	7	7
Oct. 31	Ouachita, Memphis	0	7
Nov. 7	Tulane, New Orleans	21	6
Nov. 13	Arkansas, Little Rock	13	7
Nov. 17	Texas, Austin	7	66
Nov. 20	Southwestern, Georgetown, Texas	0	18
Nov. 26	Texas A&M, Beaumont	7	14
	TOTAL POINTS:	110	125

COACH: William Driver.
CAPTAIN: Frank W. Smythe, LE.

†Known now as Arkansas State.

1915—Won 2, Lost 6

Oct. 1	Arkansas Aggies, Oxford	0	10
Oct. 8	SPU, Oxford	13	6
Oct. 15	LSU, Oxford	0	28
Oct. 23	Vanderbilt, Memphis	0	91
Oct. 30	Hendrix, Oxford	32	7
Nov. 6	Miss. A&M, Tupelo	0	65
Nov. 13	Miss. College, Jackson	6	74
Nov. 20	*Arkansas, Little Rock	—	—
Nov. 25	Alabama, Birmingham	0	53
	TOTAL POINTS:	51	334

COACH: Fred Robbins.
CAPTAIN: J. H. (Pop) Harris, T.

*Game cancelled.

1916—Won 3, Lost 6

Sept. 30	Union, Oxford	30	0
Oct. 7	Arkansas Aggies, Oxford	20	0
Oct. 14	Hendrix, Oxford	61	0
Oct. 21	Vanderbilt, Nashville	0	35
Oct. 28	Alabama, Tuscaloosa	0	27
Nov. 3	Miss. A&M, Tupelo	0	36
Nov. 11	Transylvania, Lex'ton, Ky.	3	13
Nov. 18	LSU, Baton Rouge	0	41
Nov. 30	Miss. College, Jackson	14	36
	TOTAL POINTS:	128	188

COACH: Fred Robbins.
CAPTAIN: C. Allen Anderson, C.

1917—Won 1, Lost 4, Tied 1

Oct. 6	Arkansas Aggies, Oxford	0	0
Oct. 13	LSU, Oxford	7	52
Oct. 27	Alabama, Tuscaloosa	0	54
Nov. 3	Miss. A&M, Tupelo	14	41
Nov. 10	Sewanee, Sewanee, Tenn.	7	69
Nov. 29	Miss. College, Jackson	21	0
	TOTAL POINTS:	49	216

COACH: C. R. (Dudy) Noble.
CAPTAIN: Roy Bridges, QB.

1918—Won 1, Lost 3

Nov. 9	Payne Field, West Point, Miss.	0	6
Nov. 16	Union, Oxford	39	0
Nov. 28	Miss. A&M, Starkville	0	34
Dec. 7	Miss. A&M, Oxford	0	13
	TOTAL POINTS:	39	53

COACH: C. R. (Dudy) Noble.
CAPTAIN: Edward H. Ray, HB.

1919—Won 4, Lost 4

Oct. 4	Arkansas Aggies, Oxford	32	0
Oct. 11	Alabama, Tuscaloosa	0	49
Oct. 18	LSU, Baton Rouge	0	12
Oct. 25	Tulane, New Orleans	12	27
Oct. 31	Union, Oxford	25	6
Nov. 8	Miss. A&M, Clarksdale	0	33
Nov. 15	SPU, Oxford	30	0
Nov. 27	Miss. College, Jackson	6	0
	TOTAL POINTS:	105	127

COACH: R. L. Sullivan.
CAPTAIN: Edmund Cowart, E.

1920—Won 4, Lost 3

Oct. 2	Arkansas Aggies, Oxford	33	0
Oct. 9	Ms. Normal, Hattiesburg	54	0
Oct. 16	Birmingham-Southern, Birmingham, Ala.	6	27
Oct. 23	Tulane, New Orleans	0	32
Oct. 29	Union, Oxford	86	0
Nov. 6	Miss. A&M, Greenwood	0	20
Nov. 12	SPU, Oxford	38	6
	TOTAL POINTS:	217	85

COACH: R. L. Sullivan
CAPTAIN: Rufus Creekmore, C.

1921—Won 3, Lost 6

Oct. 1	*W. Tenn. Normal, Oxford	82	0
Oct. 8	Tulane, New Orleans	0	26
Oct. 15	Millsaps, Oxford	49	0
Oct. 22	SPU, Oxford	35	0
Oct. 28	Miss. A&M, Greenwood	0	21
Nov. 5	Miss. College, Vicksburg	7	27
Nov. 12	LSU, Baton Rouge	0	21
Nov. 19	Tenn. Doctors, Memphis	6	24
Dec. 31	U. of Havana, Havana, Cuba	0	14
	TOTAL POINTS:	179	133

COACH: R. L. Sullivan.
CAPTAIN: Howard D. Robinson, FB.

*Known now as Memphis State.

1922—Won 4, Lost 5, Tied 1

Sept. 30	Union, Oxford	0	0
Oct. 7	Centre, Danville, Ky.	0	55
Oct. 14	SPU, Oxford	23	0
Oct. 21	Miss. A&M, Jackson	13	19
Oct. 28	Tennessee, Knoxville	0	49
Nov. 4	Birmingham-Sou., Oxford	6	0
Nov. 11	Hendrix, Oxford	13	7
Nov. 18	Tenn. Doctors, Memphis	0	32
Nov. 25	Camp Benning, Columbus, Ga.	13	14
Nov. 30	Millsaps, Jackson	19	7
	TOTAL POINTS:	87	183

COACH: R. A. Cowell.
CAPTAIN: Calvin C. Barbour, Jr., QB.

1923—Won 4, Lost 6

Sept. 29	Bethel College, Oxford	14	6
Oct. 6	Alabama, Tuscaloosa	0	56
Oct. 13	SPU, Oxford	33	0
Oct. 20	Miss. A&M, Jackson	6	13
Oct. 27	St. Louis U., St. Louis	3	28
Nov. 3	Birmingham-Sou., Oxford	6	0
Nov. 10	Miss. College, Meridian	0	6
Nov. 17	Tulane, New Orleans	0	19
Nov. 24	Tennessee, Knoxville	0	10
Nov. 31	Camp Benning, Columbus, Ga.	19	7
	TOTAL POINTS:	81	145

COACH: R. A. Cowell.
CAPTAIN: John T. Montgomery, HB.

1924—Won 4, Lost 5

Oct. 4	Arkansas Aggies, Oxford	10	7
Oct. 11	SPU, Oxford	7	0
Oct. 18	Miss. A&M, Jackson	0	20
Oct. 25	Arkansas, Little Rock	0	20
Nov. 1	Alabama, Montgomery	0	61
Nov. 8	Sewanee, Memphis	0	21
Nov. 15	Furman, Greenville, S.C.	2	7
Nov. 22	Ms. College, Oxford (HC)	10	6
Nov. 27	Millsaps, Jackson	7	0
	TOTAL POINTS:	36	142

COACH: Chester Barnard.
CAPTAIN: Claude Smithson, HB.

Gary Turner, defensive end

1925—Won 5, Lost 5

Sept. 26	Arkansas Aggies, Oxford	53	0
Oct. 3	Texas, Austin	0	25
Oct. 10	Tulane, New Orleans	7	26
Oct. 17	Union, Oxford	7	6
Oct. 24	Miss. A&M, Jackson	0	6
Oct. 31	Vanderbilt, Nashville	0	7
Nov. 7	Sewanee, Chattanooga	9	10
Nov. 14	Miss. College, Clinton	19	7
Nov. 21	So'western, Oxford (HC)	31	0
Nov. 26	Millsaps, Jackson	21	0
	TOTAL POINTS:	147	87

COACH: Homer Hazel.
CAPTAIN: John (Bat) Mustin, HB.

1926—Won 5, Lost 4

Sept. 25	Arkansas Aggies, Oxford	28	0
Oct. 2	Arkansas, Fayetteville	6	21
Oct. 9	Florida, Gainesville	12	7
Oct. 16	*Loyola, Oxford (HC)	13	7
Oct. 23	Drake, Des Moines, Iowa	15	33
Oct. 30	Tulane, New Orleans	0	6
Nov. 6	Southwestern, Memphis	32	27
Nov. 13	LSU, Baton Rouge	0	3
Nov. 25	Miss. A&M, Starkville	7	6
	TOTAL POINTS:	113	110

COACH: Homer Hazel.
CAPTAIN: Webster Burke, C.

*Loyola of Chicago

1927—Won 5, Lost 3, Tied 1

Sept. 24	Col. of Ozarks, Oxford	58	0
Oct. 1	Tulane, New Orleans	7	19
Oct. 7	Hendrix, Oxford	0	0
Oct. 15	Tennessee, Knoxville	7	21
Oct. 22	Southwestern, Memphis	39	0
Oct. 29	Sewanee, Sewanee, Tenn.	28	14
Nov. 5	LSU, Oxford (HC)	12	7
Nov. 11	*Loyola, Jackson	6	7
Nov. 24	Miss. A&M, Oxford	20	12
	TOTAL POINTS:	177	80

COACH: Homer Hazel.
CAPTAIN: Austin Applewhite, E.

*Loyola of Chicago.

1928 — Won 5, Lost 4

Sept. 29	Arkansas, Oxford	25	0
Oct. 6	Alabama, Tuscaloosa	0	27
Oct. 13	Tennessee, Knoxville	12	13
Oct. 20	Auburn, Birmingham	19	0
Oct. 27	*Loyola, New Orleans	14	34
Nov. 3	Clemson, Oxford (HC)	26	7
Nov. 10	LSU, Baton Rouge	6	19
Nov. 17	Southwestern, Memphis	34	2
Nov. 29	Miss. A&M, Starkville	20	19
	TOTAL POINTS:	156	121

COACH: Homer Hazel.
CAPTAIN: Thad (Pie) Vann, T.
Loyola of New Orleans.

1929 — Won 1, Lost 6, Tied 2

Sept. 28	Vanderbilt, Nashville	7	19
Oct. 5	Alabama, Tuscaloosa	7	22
Oct. 12	Tennessee, Knoxville	7	52
Oct. 18	*Loyola, New Orleans	26	24
Oct. 26	S.M.U., Dallas	0	52
Nov. 2	Sewanee, Oxford (HC)	6	6
Nov. 9	Purdue, Lafayette, Ind.	7	27
Nov. 16	LSU, Baton Rouge	6	13
Nov. 30	Miss. A&M, Oxford	7	7
	TOTAL POINTS:	73	222

COACH: Homer Hazel.
CAPTAIN: W. D. (Dump) Burnette, T.
Loyola of New Orleans (Rebels' first night game).

1930 — Won 3, Lost 5, Tied 1

Sept. 26	Union, Oxford	64	0
Oct. 4	Alabama, Tuscaloosa	0	64
Oct. 11	Tennessee, Knoxville	0	27
Oct. 18	Sewanee, Oxford (HC)	7	13
Oct. 25	Chicago U., Chicago	0	0
Nov. 1	Vanderbilt, Nashville	0	24
Nov. 8	LSU, Baton Rouge	0	6
Nov. 14	Southwestern, Oxford	37	6
Nov. 27	Miss. A&M, Starkville	20	0
	TOTAL POINTS:	128	140

COACH: Ed Walker.
CAPTAIN: Dick Peeples, E.

1931 — Won 2, Lost 6, Tied 1

Sept. 19	W. Kentucky, Oxford	13	6
Sept. 26	Tulane, New Orleans	0	31
Oct. 3	Alabama, Tuscaloosa	6	55
Oct. 10	Tennessee, Knoxville	0	38
Oct. 24	Southwestern, Memphis	20	20
Oct. 30	Marquette, Milwaukee	6	13
Nov. 7	Sewanee, Oxford (HC)	0	7
Nov. 14	LSU, Jackson	3	26
Nov. 26	Miss. A&M, Oxford	25	14
	TOTAL POINTS:	73	210

COACH: Ed Walker.
CAPTAIN: Neal Biggers, HB.

1932 — Won 5, Lost 6

Sept. 24	*Miss. Teachers, Oxford	49	0
Oct. 1	Tennessee, Knoxville	0	33
Oct. 8	Howard, Oxford	26	6
Oct. 15	Centenary, Shreveport	6	13
Oct. 22	Alabama, Tuscaloosa	13	24
Oct. 29	Auburn, Montgomery	7	14
Nov. 5	Minnesota, Minneapolis	0	26
Nov. 12	Sewanee, Oxford (HC)	27	6
Nov. 19	Southwestern, Memphis	7	0
Nov. 24	Miss. State, Starkville	13	0
Dec. 3	Tulsa, Tulsa, Okla.	0	26
	TOTAL POINTS:	148	148

COACH: Ed Walker.
CAPTAIN: Lee Trapp, G.
Known now as Southern Mississippi.

1933 — Won 6, Lost 3, Tied 2

Sept. 23	Southwestern, Memphis	6	6
Sept. 30	Miss. Teachers, Oxford	45	0
Oct. 7	Alabama, Birmingham	0	0
Oct. 14	Marquette, Milwaukee	7	0
Oct. 21	Sewanee, Oxford (HC)	41	0
Oct. 28	Clemson, Meridian	13	0
Nov. 4	Birmingham-Southern, Oxford	12	0
Nov. 11	Tennessee, Knoxville	6	35
Nov. 18	LSU, Baton Rouge	0	31
Nov. 25	Centenary, Jackson	6	7
Dec. 2	Miss. State, Oxford	31	0
	TOTAL POINTS:	167	79

COACH: Ed Walker.
CAPTAIN: Appointed.

1934 — Won 4, Lost 5, Tied 1

Sept. 29	*W. Tenn. Teachers, Oxford	44	0
Oct. 5	†Southwestern, Clarksdale	19	0
Oct. 13	Tennessee, Knoxville	0	27
Oct. 20	Howard, Oxford	6	7
Oct. 27	Sewanee, Oxford (HC)	19	6
Nov. 3	Tulane, New Orleans	0	15
Nov. 10	Florida, Gainesville	13	13
Nov. 17	LSU, Jackson	0	14
Nov. 24	Centenary, Shreveport	6	13
Dec. 1	Miss. State, Jackson	7	3
	TOTAL POINTS:	114	98

COACH: Ed Walker.
CAPTAIN: Appointed.
Known now as Memphis State.
†Night Game.*

Raymond Brown, quarterback, M.V.P 1958 Sugar Bowl

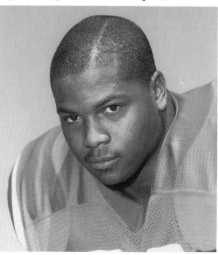

Jeff Herrod, All-SEC Linebacker

1935 — Won 9, Lost 3

Sept. 20	†Millsaps, Jackson	20	0
Sept. 28	W. Tenn. Teachers, Campus	92	0
Oct. 5	Southwestern, Oxford	33	0
Oct. 11	†Sewanee, Clarksdale	33	0
Oct. 19	Florida, Oxford (HC)	27	6
Oct. 26	Marquette, Milwaukee	7	33
Nov. 1	†St. Louis U., St. Louis	21	7
Nov. 9	Tennessee, Memphis	13	14
Nov. 16	Centre, Danville, Ky.	26	0
Nov. 23	Centenary, Jackson	6	0
Nov. 30	Miss. State, Oxford	14	6
	ORANGE BOWL, Miami		
1-1-36	Catholic University	19	20
	TOTAL POINTS:	311	86

COACH: Ed Walker.
CAPTAIN: Appointed.
†Night Game.*

1936 — Won 5, Lost 5, Tied 2

Sept. 19	Union, Oxford	45	0
Sept. 26	Tulane, New Orleans	6	7
Oct. 2	†Temple, Philadelphia	7	12
Oct. 9	†Geo. Washington, Washington	0	0
Oct. 17	†LSU, Baton Rouge	0	13
Oct. 24	Catholic U., Oxford (HC)	14	0
Oct. 31	Centenary, Shreveport	24	7
Nov. 7	*Loyola, Oxford	34	0
Nov. 14	Marquette, Milwaukee	0	33
Nov. 21	Miss. State, Starkville	6	26
Nov. 27	†Miami U., Miami, Fla.	14	0
Dec. 5	Tennessee, Memphis	0	0
	TOTAL POINTS:	150	98

COACH: Ed Walker.
CAPTAIN: Marvin L. Hutson, C.
†Night Game.*
Loyola of New Orleans.

1937 — Won 4, Lost 5, Tied 1

Sept. 25	Louisiana Tech, Oxford	13	0
Oct. 1	†Temple, Philadelphia	0	0
Oct. 9	St. Louis U., Oxford (HC)	21	0
Oct. 16	†LSU, Baton Rouge	0	13
Oct. 23	Ouachita, Oxford	46	0
Oct. 30	Tulane, New Orleans	7	14
Nov. 5	Geo. Washington, Washington	27	6
Nov. 13	Arkansas, Memphis	6	32
Nov. 25	Miss. State, Oxford	7	9
Dec. 4	Tennessee, Memphis	0	32
	TOTAL POINTS:	127	106

COACH: Ed Walker.
CAPTAIN: Frank M. (Bruiser) Kinard, LT.
†Night Game.*

1938 — Won 9, Lost 2

Sept. 24	†LSU, Baton Rouge	20	7
Oct. 1	Louisiana Tech, Oxford	27	7
Oct. 8	Miss. Teachers, Oxford	14	0
Oct. 15	Vanderbilt, Nashville	7	13
Oct. 22	Centenary, Oxford (HC)	47	14
Oct. 29	†Geo. Washington, Washington	25	0
Nov. 5	St. Louis U., St. Louis	14	12
Nov. 12	Sewanee, Oxford	39	0
Nov. 19	Arkansas, Memphis	20	14
Nov. 26	Miss. State, Starkville	19	6
Dec. 3	Tennessee, Memphis	0	47
	TOTAL POINTS:	232	120

COACH: Harry J. Mehre.
CAPTAIN: Kimble Bradley, QB.
†Night Game.*

1939 — Won 7, Lost 2

Sept. 30	†LSU, Baton Rouge	14	7
Oct. 7	Southwestern, Memphis	41	0
Oct. 14	†Centenary, Shreveport	34	0
Oct. 21	St. Louis U., Oxford (HC)	42	0
Oct. 28	Tulane, New Orleans	6	18
Nov. 4	Vanderbilt, Memphis	14	7
Nov. 11	Miss. Teachers, Hattiesburg	27	7
Nov. 18	W. Tenn. Teachers, Oxford	46	7
Nov. 25	Miss. State, Oxford	6	18
	TOTAL POINTS:	230	64

COACH: Harry J. Mehre.
CAPTAIN: Bill Schneller, QB.

†Night Game.

1940 — Won 9, Lost 2

Sept. 21	Union, Oxford	37	0
Sept. 28	†LSU, Baton Rouge	19	6
Oct. 5	Southwestern, Memphis	27	6
Oct. 12	Georgia, Athens	28	14
Oct. 19	Duquesne, Oxford (HC)	14	6
Oct. 26	Arkansas, Memphis	20	21
Nov. 2	Vanderbilt, Nashville	13	7
Nov. 9	Holy Cross, Worcester	34	7
Nov. 16	W. Tenn. Teachers, Oxford	38	7
Nov. 23	Miss. State, Starkville	0	19
Nov. 29	†Miami U., Miami, Fla.	21	7
	TOTAL POINTS:	251	100

COACH: Harry J. Mehre.
CAPTAIN: George Kinard, LG.

†Night Game.

1941 — Won 6, Lost 2, Tied 1

Sept. 26	†Georgetown, Washington	6	16
Oct. 4	Southwestern, Oxford (HC)	27	0
Oct. 10	†Georgia, Athens	14	14
Oct. 18	Holy Cross, Worcester	21	0
Oct. 25	Tulane, New Orleans	20	13
Nov. 1	Marquette, Milwaukee	12	6
Nov. 8	†LSU, Baton Rouge	13	12
Nov. 22	Arkansas, Memphis	18	0
Nov. 29	Miss. State, Oxford	0	6
	TOTAL POINTS:	131	67

COACH: Harry J. Mehre.
CO-CAPTAINS: J. W. (Wobble) Davidson, LE; Homer Larry Hazel, LG.

†Night Game.

1942 — Won 2, Lost 7

Sept. 26	W. Ky. Teachers, Oxford	39	6
Oct. 2	Georgetown, Washington	6	14
Oct. 10	Georgia, Memphis	13	48
Oct. 17	†LSU, Baton Rouge	7	21
Oct. 24	Arkansas, Memphis	6	7
Oct. 31	Memphis State, Oxford	48	0
Nov. 7	Vanderbilt, Memphis	0	19
Nov. 14	Tennessee, Memphis	0	14
Nov. 21	Miss. State, Starkville	13	34
	TOTAL POINTS:	132	163

COACH: Harry J. Mehre.
CAPTAIN: Dan Wood, C.

1943

Football Abolished at all Mississippi State-Supported Institutions by Board of Trustees.

1944 — Won 2, Lost 6

Sept. 23	†Kentucky, Lexington	7	27
Sept. 30	†Florida, Jacksonville	26	6
Oct. 7	†Tennessee, Memphis	7	20
Oct. 21	Tulsa, Memphis	0	47
Oct. 28	Arkansas, Memphis	18	26
Nov. 4	Jackson AAB, Oxford	0	10
Nov. 11	Alabama, Mobile	6	34
Nov. 25	Miss. State, Oxford	13	8
	TOTAL POINTS:	77	178

COACH: Harry J. Mehre.
CAPTAIN: Bob McCain, LE.

†Night Game.

1945 — Won 4, Lost 5

Sept. 21	†Kentucky, Memphis	21	7
Sept. 29	†Florida, Jacksonville	13	26
Oct. 6	Vanderbilt, Nashville	14	7
Oct. 13	Louisiana Tech, Oxford	26	21
Oct. 27	Arkansas, Memphis	0	19
Nov. 3	†LSU, Baton Rouge	13	32
Nov. 10	Tennessee, Memphis	0	34
Nov. 24	Miss. State, Starkville	7	6
Nov. 29	Chattanooga, Chattanooga	6	31
	TOTAL POINTS:	100	183

COACH: Harry J. Mehre.
CAPTAIN: Bob McCain, LE-HB.

†Night Game.

1946 — Won 2, Lost 7

Sept. 21	†Kentucky, Lexington	6	20
Sept. 28	†Florida, Jacksonville	13	7
Oct. 5	Vanderbilt, Memphis	0	7
Oct. 12	Georgia Tech, Atlanta	7	24
Oct. 19	La. Tech, Oxford (HC)	6	7
Oct. 26	Arkansas, Memphis	9	7
Nov. 2	†LSU, Baton Rouge	21	34
Nov. 9	Tennessee, Memphis	14	18
Nov. 23	Miss. State, Oxford	0	20
	TOTAL POINTS:	76	144

COACH: Harold (Red) Drew.
CAPTAIN: Ray Poole, RE.

†Night Game.

1947 — Won 9, Lost 2

SEC CHAMPIONS

Sept. 20	Kentucky, Oxford (HC)	14	7
Sept. 27	†Florida, Jacksonville	14	6
Oct. 4	South Carolina, Memphis	33	0
Oct. 11	Vanderbilt, Nashville	6	10
Oct. 18	Tulane, New Orleans	27	14
Oct. 25	Arkansas, Memphis	14	19
Nov. 1	†LSU, Baton Rouge	20	18
Nov. 8	Tennessee, Memphis	43	13
Nov. 15	Chattanooga, Oxford	52	0
Nov. 29	Miss. State, Starkville	33	14
	DELTA BOWL, Memphis		
1-1-48	Texas Christian	13	9
	TOTAL POINTS:	269	110

COACH: John H. Vaught.
CAPTAIN: Charlie Conerly, LHB.

†Night Game.

1948 — Won 8, Lost 1

Sept. 25	†Florida, Gainesville	14	0
Oct. 2	†Kentucky, Lexington	20	7
Oct. 9	Vanderbilt, Oxford (HC)	20	7
Oct. 16	Tulane, New Orleans	7	20
Oct. 23	Boston College, Memphis	32	13
Oct. 30	†LSU, Baton Rouge	49	19
Nov. 6	Chattanooga, Chattanooga	34	7
Nov. 13	Tennessee, Memphis	16	13
Nov. 27	Miss. State, Oxford	34	7
	TOTAL POINTS:	226	93

COACH: John H. Vaught.
CAPTAIN: Doug Hamley, RT.

†Night Game.

1949 — Won 4, Lost 5, Tied 1

Sept. 16	†Memphis State, Memphis	40	7
Sept. 23	†Auburn, Montgomery	40	7
Oct. 1	Kentucky, Oxford (HC)	0	47
Oct. 8	Vanderbilt, Nashville	27	28
Oct. 14	†Boston College, Boston	25	25
Oct. 22	†Texas Christian, Fort Worth	27	33
Oct. 29	†LSU, Baton Rouge	7	34
Nov. 5	Chattanooga, Oxford	47	27
Nov. 12	Tennessee, Memphis	7	35
Nov. 26	Miss. State, Starkville	26	0
	TOTAL POINTS:	246	243

COACH: John H. Vaught.
CAPTAIN: Roland Dale, LT.

†Night Game.

1950 — Won 5, Lost 5

Sept. 22	†Memphis State, Memphis	39	7
Sept. 30	†Kentucky, Lexington	0	27
Oct. 7	Boston College, Oxford (HC)	54	0
Oct. 14	Vanderbilt, Nashville	14	20
Oct. 21	Tulane, New Orleans	20	27
Oct. 28	Texas Christian, Memphis	19	7
Nov. 4	†LSU, Baton Rouge	14	40
Nov. 11	Chattanooga, Oxford	20	0
Nov. 18	Tennessee, Knoxville	0	35
Dec. 2	Miss. State, Oxford	27	20
	TOTAL POINTS:	207	183

COACH: John H. Vaught.
CAPTAIN: Ken Farragut, C.

†Night Game.

1951 — Won 6, Lost 3, Tied 1

Sept. 21	†Memphis State, Memphis	32	0
Sept. 29	Kentucky, Oxford	21	17
Oct. 5	†Boston College, Memphis	34	7
Oct. 13	Vanderbilt, Memphis	20	34
Oct. 20	Tulane, Oxford (HC)	25	6
Oct. 26	†Miami U., Miami, Fla.	7	20
Nov. 3	†LSU, Baton Rouge	6	6
Nov. 10	Auburn, Mobile	39	14
Nov. 17	Tennessee, Oxford	21	46
Dec. 1	Miss. State, Starkville	49	7
	TOTAL POINTS:	254	157

COACH: John H. Vaught.
CAPTAIN: Othar Crawford, LG.

†Night Game.

1952 — Won 8, Lost 1, Tied 2

Sept. 19	†Memphis State, Memphis	54	6
Sept. 27	Kentucky, Lexington	13	13
Oct. 4	Auburn, Memphis	20	7
Oct. 11	Vanderbilt, Nashville	21	21
Oct. 18	Tulane, New Orleans	20	14
Oct. 25	Arkansas, Little Rock	34	7
Nov. 1	LSU, Oxford (HC)	28	0
Nov. 8	†Houston, Houston, Tex.	6	0
Nov. 15	Maryland, Oxford	21	14
Nov. 29	Miss. State, Oxford	20	14
	SUGAR BOWL, New Orleans		
1-1-53	‡Georgia Tech	7	24
	TOTAL POINTS:	244	120

COACH: John H. Vaught.
CO-CAPTAINS: Kline Gilbert, RT; Jim Ingram, C.

†Night Game.   ‡TV Game.

Freddie Joe Nunn, defensive end/linebacker

1953 — Won 7, Lost 2, Tied 1

Sept. 19	Chattanooga, Jackson	39	6
Sept. 26	Kentucky, Oxford	22	6
Oct. 3	Auburn, Auburn, Ala.	0	13
Oct. 10	Vanderbilt, Oxford (HC)	28	6
Oct. 17	Tulane, New Orleans	45	14
Oct. 24	‡Arkansas, Memphis	28	0
Oct. 31	†LSU, Baton Rouge	27	16
Nov. 7	North Texas State, Oxford	40	7
Nov. 14	Maryland, College Park	0	38
Nov. 28	Miss. State, Starkville	7	7
	TOTAL POINTS:	236	113

COACH: John H. Vaught.
CAPTAIN: Ed Beatty, C.

†Night Game.   ‡TV Game.

1954 — Won 9, Lost 2

SEC CHAMPIONS

Sept. 17	†No. Texas State, Memphis	35	12
Sept. 25	†Kentucky, Memphis	28	9
Oct. 2	†Villanova, Philadelphia	52	0
Oct. 9	†Vanderbilt, Nashville	22	7
Oct. 16	Tulane, Oxford (HC)	34	7
Oct. 23	Arkansas, Little Rock	0	6
Oct. 30	†LSU, Baton Rouge	21	6
Nov. 6	Memphis State, Memphis	51	0
Nov. 13	†Houston, Houston	26	0
Nov. 27	Miss. State, Oxford	14	0
	SUGAR BOWL, New Orleans		
1-1-55	‡Navy	0	21
	TOTAL POINTS:	283	68

COACH: John H. Vaught.
CO-CAPTAINS: Jimmy Patton, LHB; Allen (Red) Muirhead, RHB.

†Night Game.   ‡TV Game.

1955 — Won 10, Lost 1

SEC CHAMPIONS

Sept. 17	†Georgia, Atlanta	26	13
Sept. 24	†Kentucky, Lexington	14	21
Oct. 1	North Texas State, Oxford	33	0
Oct. 8	†Vanderbilt, Memphis	13	0
Oct. 15	Tulane, New Orleans	27	13
Oct. 22	Arkansas, Oxford (HC)	17	7
Oct. 29	†LSU, Baton Rouge	29	26
Nov. 5	†Memphis State, Memphis	39	6
Nov. 12	†Houston, Jackson	27	11
Nov. 26	Miss. State, Starkville	26	0
	COTTON BOWL, Dallas		
1-2-56	‡Texas Christian	14	13
	TOTAL POINTS:	265	110

COACH: John H. Vaught.
CAPTAIN: Vaughn (Buddy) Alliston, LG.

†Night Game.   ‡TV Game.

1956 — Won 7, Lost 3

Sept. 22	North Texas State, Oxford	45	0
Sept. 29	†Kentucky, Memphis	37	7
Oct. 6	†Houston, Jackson	14	0
Oct. 13	Vanderbilt, Oxford (HC)	16	0
Oct. 20	†Tulane, Jackson	3	10
Oct. 27	†Arkansas, Little Rock	0	14
Nov. 3	†LSU, Baton Rouge	46	17
Nov. 10	Memphis State, Memphis	26	0
Nov. 17	Tennessee, Knoxville	7	27
Dec. 1	Miss. State, Oxford	13	7
	TOTAL POINTS:	207	82

COACH: John H. Vaught.
CAPTAIN: Appointed.

†Night Game.

1957 — Won 9, Lost 1, Tied 1

Sept. 21	Trinity, San Antonio	44	0
Sept. 28	†Kentucky, Lexington	15	0
Oct. 5	Hardin-Simmons, Oxford	34	7
Oct. 12	†Vanderbilt, Nashville	28	0
Oct. 18	†Tulane, New Orleans	50	0
Oct. 26	Arkansas, Memphis	6	12
Nov. 2	†Houston, Jackson	20	7
Nov. 9	LSU, Oxford (HC)	14	12
Nov. 16	Tennessee, Memphis	14	7
Nov. 30	Miss. State, Starkville	7	7
	SUGAR BOWL, New Orleans		
1-1-58	‡Texas	39	7
	TOTAL POINTS:	271	59

COACH: John H. Vaught.
CO-CAPTAINS: Jackie Simpson, LG; Gene Hickerson, RT.

†Night Game.   ‡TV Game.

1958 — Won 9, Lost 2

Sept. 20	†Memphis State, Memphis	17	0
Sept. 27	†Kentucky, Memphis	27	6
Oct. 4	†Trinity, San Antonio	21	0
Oct. 11	†Tulane, New Orleans	19	8
Oct. 18	Hardin-Simmons, Oxford	24	0
Oct. 25	Arkansas, Little Rock	14	12
Nov. 1	†LSU, Baton Rouge	0	14
Nov. 8	Houston, Oxford (HC)	56	7
Nov. 15	Tennessee, Knoxville	16	18
Nov. 29	Miss. State, Oxford	21	0
	GATOR BOWL, Jacksonville		
Dec. 27	‡Florida	7	3
	TOTAL POINTS:	222	68

COACH: John H. Vaught.
CO-CAPTAINS: Milton Crain, C; Kent Lovelace, RHB.

†Night Game.   ‡TV Game.

1959 — Won 10, Lost 1

SEC TEAM OF THE DECADE

Sept. 19	†Houston, Houston, Tex.	16	0
Sept. 26	†Kentucky, Lexington	16	0
Oct. 3	Memphis State, Memphis	43	0
Oct. 10	†Vanderbilt, Nashville	33	0
Oct. 17	Tulane, Oxford (HC)	53	7
Oct. 24	Arkansas, Memphis	28	0
Oct. 31	LSU, Baton Rouge	3	7
Nov. 7	Chattanooga, Oxford	58	0
Nov. 14	Tennessee, Memphis	37	7
Nov. 28	Miss. State, Starkville	42	0
	SUGAR BOWL, New Orleans		
1-1-60	‡LSU	21	0
	TOTAL POINTS:	350	21

COACH: John H. Vaught.
CO-CAPTAINS: Ken Kirk, C; Charlie Flowers, FB.

†Night Game.   ‡TV Game.

Everett Lindsay, All-America offensive guard

1960 — Won 10, Lost 0, Tied 1

FWAA NATIONAL CHAMPIONS
SEC CHAMPIONS

Sept. 17	†Houston, Houston, Tex.	42	0
Sept. 24	†Kentucky, Memphis	21	6
Oct. 1	Memphis State, Memphis	31	20
Oct. 8	†Vanderbilt, Nashville	26	0
Oct. 15	†Tulane, New Orleans	26	13
Oct. 22	†Arkansas, Little Rock	10	7
Oct. 29	‡LSU, Oxford (HC)	6	6
Nov. 5	Chattanooga, Oxford	45	0
Nov. 12	Tennessee, Knoxville	24	3
Nov. 26	Miss. State, Oxford	35	9
	SUGAR BOWL, New Orleans		
1-2-61	‡Rice	14	6
	TOTAL POINTS:	280	70

COACH: John H. Vaught.
CO-CAPTAINS: Jake Gibbs, QB; Warner Alford, LG.

†Night Game.   ‡TV Game.

1961 — Won 9, Lost 2

Sept. 23	‡Arkansas, Jackson	16	0
Sept. 30	†Kentucky, Lexington	20	6
Oct. 7	Florida State, Oxford	33	0
Oct. 14	Houston, Memphis	47	7
Oct. 21	†Tulane, Jackson	41	0
Oct. 28	Vanderbilt, Oxford (HC)	47	0
Nov. 4	†LSU, Baton Rouge	7	10
Nov. 11	Chattanooga, Oxford	54	0
Nov. 18	Tennessee, Memphis	24	10
Dec. 2	Miss. State, Starkville	37	7
	COTTON BOWL, Dallas		
1-1-62	‡Texas	7	12
	TOTAL POINTS:	333	52

COACH: John H. Vaught.
TRI-CAPTAINS: Doug Elmore, QB; Billy Ray Jones, LG; Ralph Smith, LE.

†Night Game.   ‡TV Game.

1962 – Won 10, Lost 0

SEC CHAMPIONS
PERFECT SEASON

Sept. 22	†Memphis State, Memphis	21	7
Sept. 29	†Kentucky, Jackson	14	0
Oct. 6	Houston, Jackson	40	7
Oct. 20	†Tulane, Jackson	21	0
Oct. 27	†Vanderbilt, Memphis	35	0
Nov. 3	†LSU, Baton Rouge	15	7
Nov. 10	Chattanooga, Oxford	52	7
Nov. 17	Tennessee, Knoxville	19	6
Dec. 1	Miss. State, Oxford	13	6
	SUGAR BOWL, New Orleans		
1-1-63	‡Arkansas	17	13
	TOTAL POINTS:	247	53

COACH: John H. Vaught.
CO-CAPTAINS: Glynn Griffing, QB; Louis Guy, WB.

†*Night Game.*   ‡*TV Game.*

1963 – Won 7, Lost 1, Tied 2

SEC CHAMPIONS

Sept. 21	†Memphis State, Memphis	0	0
Sept. 28	†Kentucky, Lexington	31	7
Oct. 5	†Houston, Houston	20	6
Oct. 19	Tulane, New Orleans	21	0
Oct. 26	Vanderbilt, Oxford (HC)	27	7
Nov. 2	‡LSU, Baton Rouge	37	3
Nov. 9	Tampa, Oxford	41	0
Nov. 16	Tennessee, Memphis	20	0
Nov. 30	Miss. State, Starkville	10	10
	SUGAR BOWL, New Orleans		
1-1-64	‡Alabama	7	12
	TOTAL POINTS:	214	45

COACH: John H. Vaught.
CO-CAPTAINS: Kenny Dill, C; Whaley Hall, T.

†*Night Game.*   ‡*TV Game.*

1964 – Won 5, Lost 5, Tied 1

Sept. 19	Memphis State, Oxford	30	0
Sept. 26	Kentucky, Jackson	21	27
Oct. 3	Houston, Oxford (HC)	31	9
Oct. 10	Florida, Gainesville	14	30
Oct. 17	†Tulane, New Orleans	14	9
Oct. 24	†Vanderbilt, Nashville	7	7
Oct. 31	†LSU, Baton Rouge	10	11
Nov. 7	Tampa, Oxford	36	0
Nov. 14	Tennessee, Knoxville	30	0
Dec. 5	‡Miss. State, Oxford	17	20
	BLUEBONNET BOWL, Houston		
Dec. 19	‡Tulsa	7	14
	TOTAL POINTS:	217	127

COACH: John H. Vaught.
CO-CAPTAINS: Bobby Robinson, LG; Allen Brown, LE.

†*Night Game.*   ‡*TV Game.*

Randy Baldwin, tailback

1965 – Won 7, Lost 4

Sept. 18	†Memphis State, Memphis	34	14
Sept. 25	†Kentucky, Lexington	7	16
Oct. 2	†Alabama, Birmingham	16	17
Oct. 9	Florida, Oxford (HC)	0	17
Oct. 16	†Tulane, Jackson	24	7
Oct. 23	Vanderbilt, Oxford	24	7
Oct. 30	LSU, Jackson	23	0
Nov. 6	†Houston, Houston, Tex.	3	17
Nov. 13	‡Tennessee, Memphis	14	13
Nov. 27	Miss. State, Starkville	21	0
	LIBERTY BOWL, Memphis		
Dec. 18	‡Auburn	13	7
	TOTAL POINTS:	179	115

COACH: John H. Vaught.
CO-CAPTAINS: Mike Dennis, TB; Stan Hindman, G.

†*Night Game.*   ‡*TV Game.*

1966 – Won 8, Lost 3

Sept. 17	†Memphis State, Memphis	13	0
Sept. 24	†Kentucky, Jackson	17	0
Oct. 1	Alabama, Jackson	7	17
Oct. 8	Georgia, Athens	3	9
Oct. 15	So. Miss., Oxford (HC)	14	7
Oct. 22	Houston, Memphis	27	6
Oct. 29	†LSU, Baton Rouge	17	0
Nov. 12	Tennessee, Knoxville	14	7
Nov. 19	Vanderbilt, Jackson	34	0
Nov. 26	Miss. State, Oxford	24	0
	BLUEBONNET BOWL, Houston		
Dec. 17	‡Texas	0	19
	TOTAL POINTS:	170	65

COACH: John H. Vaught.
CO-CAPTAINS: Doug Cunningham, TB; Chuck Hinton, C.

†*Night Game.*   ‡*TV Game.*

1967 – Won 6, Lost 4, Tied 1

Sept. 23	†Memphis State, Memphis	17	27
Sept. 30	†Kentucky, Lexington	26	13
Oct. 7	Alabama, Birmingham	7	21
Oct. 14	†Georgia, Jackson	29	20
Oct. 21	So. Miss., Oxford (HC)	23	14
Oct. 28	Houston, Oxford	14	13
Nov. 4	‡LSU, Jackson	13	13
Nov. 18	Tennessee, Memphis	7	20
Nov. 25	Vanderbilt, Nashville	28	7
Dec. 2	Miss. State, Starkville	10	3
	SUN BOWL, El Paso		
Dec. 30	‡Texas, El Paso	7	14
	TOTAL POINTS:	181	165

COACH: John H. Vaught.
CO-CAPTAINS: Michel (Mac) Haik, SE; Dan Sartin, DT.

†*Night Game.*   ‡*TV Game.*

1968 – Won 7, Lost 3, Tied 1

Sept. 21	†Memphis State, Memphis	21	7
Sept. 28	†Kentucky, Jackson	30	14
Oct. 5	Alabama, Jackson	10	8
Oct. 12	‡Georgia, Athens	7	21
Oct. 19	So. Miss., Oxford (HC)	21	13
Oct. 26	Houston, Jackson	7	29
Nov. 2	†LSU, Baton Rouge	27	24
Nov. 9	Chattanooga, Oxford	38	16
Nov. 16	Tennessee, Knoxville	0	31
Nov. 30	Miss. State, Oxford	17	17
	LIBERTY BOWL, Memphis		
Dec. 14	‡Virginia Tech	34	17
	TOTAL POINTS:	212	197

COACH: John H. Vaught
CO-CAPTAINS: H. N. (Hank) Shows, TE; Robert Bailey, MM.

†*Night Game.*   ‡*TV Game.*

1969 – Won 8, Lost 3

Sept. 20	Memphis State, Oxford	28	3
Sept. 27	Kentucky, Lexington	9	10
Oct. 4	†‡Alabama, Birmingham	32	33
Oct. 11	Georgia, Jackson	25	17
Oct. 18	So. Miss., Oxford (HC)	69	7
Oct. 25	†Houston, Houston	11	25
Nov. 1	‡LSU, Jackson	26	23
Nov. 8	Chattanooga, Oxford	21	0
Nov. 15	Tennessee, Jackson	38	0
Nov. 27	Miss. State, Starkville	48	22
	SUGAR BOWL, New Orleans		
1-1-70	Arkansas	27	22
	TOTAL POINTS:	334	162

COACH: John H. Vaught.
CO-CAPTAINS: Bo Bowen, FB; Glenn Cannon, S.

†*Night Game.*   ‡*TV Game.*

1970 – Won 7, Lost 4

Sept. 19	†Memphis State, Memphis	47	13
Sept. 26	Kentucky, Jackson	20	17
Oct. 3	†‡Alabama, Jackson	48	23
Oct. 10	Georgia, Athens	31	21
Oct. 17	So. Miss., Oxford	14	30
Oct. 24	†Vanderbilt, Nashville	26	16
Nov. 7	Houston, Oxford (HC)	24	13
Nov. 14	Chattanooga, Oxford	44	7
Nov. 26	Miss. State, Oxford	14	19
Dec. 5	†‡LSU, Baton Rouge	17	61
	GATOR BOWL, Jacksonville		
1-2-71	‡Auburn	28	35
	TOTAL POINTS:	313	255

COACH: John H. Vaught.
CO-CAPTAINS: Archie Manning, QB; Dennis Coleman, DE.

†*Night Game.*   ‡*TV Game.*

1971 – Won 10, Lost 2

Sept. 11	†Long Beach State, Jackson	29	13
Sept. 18	†Memphis State, Memphis	49	21
Sept. 25	Kentucky, Lexington	34	20
Oct. 2	Alabama, Birmingham	6	40
Oct. 9	Georgia, Jackson	7	38
Oct. 16	So. Miss., Oxford	20	6
Oct. 23	Vanderbilt, Oxford (HC)	28	7
Oct. 30	LSU, Jackson	24	22
Nov. 6	†Tampa, Tampa, Fla.	28	27
Nov. 13	Chattanooga, Oxford	49	10
Nov. 25	Miss. State, Starkville	48	0
	PEACH BOWL, Atlanta		
Dec. 30	†‡Georgia Tech	41	18
	TOTAL POINTS:	363	222

COACH: Billy R. Kinard.
CO-CAPTAINS: Riley Myers, SE; Paul Dongieux, LB.

†*Night Game.*   ‡*TV Game.*

1972 – Won 5, Lost 5

Sept. 16	†Memphis State, Memphis	34	29
Sept. 23	†South Carolina, Columbia	21	0
Sept. 30	Southern Miss., Oxford	13	9
Oct. 7	Auburn, Jackson	13	19
Oct. 14	Georgia, Jackson	13	14
Oct. 21	Florida, Oxford (HC)	0	16
Oct. 28	Vanderbilt, Nashville	31	7
Nov. 4	†LSU, Baton Rouge	16	17
Nov. 18	Tennessee, Knoxville	0	17
Nov. 25	Miss. State, Oxford	51	14
	TOTAL POINTS:	192	142

COACH: Billy R. Kinard.
CO-CAPTAINS: Don Leathers, OT; Reggie Dill, DE.

†*Night Game.*

1992 OLE MISS FOOTBALL STAFF—Front row, from left: Leroy Mullins, Melvin Smith, Jim Carmody, head coach Billy Brewer, Joe Lee Dunn, Larry Beckish, and Blake Barnes. Back row, from left: Gary Withrow, John Neal, Chuck Okey, Ken Matous, Joe Wickline, Freeman Horton, and Keith Daniels.

1973 — Won 6, Lost 5

Sept. 8 †Villanova, Jackson	24	6
Sept. 15 Missouri, Columbia	0	17
Sept. 22 Memphis State, Jackson	13	17
Sept. 29 Southern Miss., Oxford	41	0
Oct. 6 Auburn, Auburn	7	14
Oct. 13 Georgia, Athens	0	20
Oct. 20 Florida, Gainesville	13	10
Oct. 27 Vanderbilt, Oxford (HC)	24	14
Nov. 3 ‡LSU, Jackson	14	51
Nov. 17 ‡Tennessee, Jackson	28	18
Nov. 24 Miss. State, Jackson	38	10
TOTAL POINTS:	202	177

COACHES: Billy R. Kinard; John H. Vaught.
CO-CAPTAINS: Norris Weese, QB; Jim Stuart, MLB.

†Night Game.   ‡TV Game.

1974 — Won 3, Lost 8

Sept. 14 †Missouri, Jackson	10	0
Sept. 21 †Memphis State, Memphis	7	15
Sept. 28 So. Miss., Oxford	20	14
Oct. 5 ‡Alabama, Jackson	21	35
Oct. 12 Georgia, Athens	0	49
Oct. 19 So. Carolina, Oxford (HC)	7	10
Oct. 26 Vanderbilt, Nashville	14	24
Nov. 2 †LSU, Baton Rouge	0	24
Nov. 16 Tennessee, Memphis	17	29
Nov. 23 Miss. State, Jackson	13	31
Nov. 30 Tulane, New Orleans	26	10
TOTAL POINTS:	135	241

COACH: Ken Cooper.
TRI-CAPTAINS: Dick Lawrence, OT; Stump Russell, LB; Kenny King, LB.

†Night Game.   ‡TV Game.

1975 — Won 6, Lost 5

Sept. 6 †Baylor, Waco	10	20
Sept. 13 Texas A&M, College Station	0	7
Sept. 20 †Tulane, New Orleans	3	14
Sept. 27 Southern Miss., Oxford	24	8
Oct. 4 Alabama, Birmingham	6	32
Oct. 11 Georgia, Oxford (HC)	28	13
Oct. 18 South Carolina, Jackson	29	35
Oct. 25 Vanderbilt, Oxford	17	7
Nov. 1 ‡LSU, Jackson	17	13
Nov. 15 Tennessee, Memphis	23	6
Nov. 22 Miss. State, Jackson	13	7
TOTAL POINTS:	170	162

COACH: Ken Cooper.
TRI-CAPTAINS: Paul Hofer, FB; Ben Williams, MG; Kenny King, LB.

†Night Game.   ‡TV Game.

1976 — Won 6, Lost 5

Sept. 4 †Memphis State, Memphis	16	21
Sept. 11 †Alabama, Jackson	10	7
Sept. 18 Tulane, Oxford	34	7
Sept. 25 †So. Miss., Hattiesburg	28	0
Oct. 2 Auburn, Jackson	0	10
Oct. 9 Georgia, Oxford (HC)	21	17
Oct. 16 †So. Carolina, Columbia	7	10
Oct. 23 Vanderbilt, Nashville	20	3
Oct. 30 †LSU, Baton Rouge	0	45
Nov. 13 Tennessee, Knoxville	6	32
Nov. 20 *Miss. State, Jackson	11	28
TOTAL POINTS:	153	180

*Won by forfeit.

COACH: Ken Cooper.
CAPTAINS: Wade Griffin, TE; George Stuart, LB; Reggie Pace, C.

†Night Game.

1977 — Won 6, Lost 5

Sept. 3 †Memphis St., Jackson	7	3
Sept. 10 †Alabama, Birmingham	13	34
Sept. 17 Notre Dame, Jackson	20	13
Sept. 24 So. Miss., Oxford	19	27
Oct. 1 ‡Auburn, Auburn	15	21
Oct. 8 Georgia, Athens	13	14
Oct. 15 So. Carolina, Oxford	17	10
Oct. 22 Vanderbilt, Oxford (HC)	26	14
Oct. 29 ‡LSU, Jackson	21	28
Nov. 12 Tennessee, Memphis	43	14
Nov. 19 *Miss. State, Jackson	14	18
TOTAL POINTS:	208	196

*Won by forfeit.

COACH: Ken Cooper.
TRI-CAPTAINS: George Plasketes, DE; Randy White, OG; Bob Lewis, C.

†Night Game.   ‡TV Game.

1978 — Won 5, Lost 6

Sept. 9 †Memphis State, Jackson	14	7
Sept. 23 Missouri, Columbia	14	45
Sept. 30 †So. Miss., Jackson	16	13
Oct. 7 Georgia, Athens	3	42
Oct. 14 Kentucky, Oxford (HC)	17	24
Oct. 21 So. Carolina, Columbia	17	18
Oct. 28 Vanderbilt, Nashville	35	10
Nov. 4 ‡LSU, Baton Rouge	8	30
Nov. 11 Tulane, Oxford	13	3
Nov. 18 Tennessee, Knoxville	17	41
Nov. 25 Miss. State, Jackson	27	7
TOTAL POINTS:	181	240

COACH: Steve Sloan.
CO-CAPTAINS: Curtis Weathers, SE; Lawrence Johnson, DT; Bobby Garner, QB.

†Night Game.   ‡TV Game.

Andre Townsend, All-SEC defensive end

1979 — Won 4, Lost 7

Sept. 15	†Memphis State, Memphis	38	34
Sept. 22	‡Missouri, Jackson	7	33
Sept. 29	†So. Miss., Jackson	8	38
Oct. 6	Georgia, Oxford	21	24
Oct. 13	†Kentucky, Lexington	3	14
Oct. 20	†So. Carolina, Columbia	14	21
Oct. 27	Vanderbilt, Oxford (HC)	63	28
Nov. 3	LSU, Jackson	24	28
Nov. 10	‡Tulane, New Orleans	15	49
Nov. 17	Tennessee, Jackson	44	20
Nov. 24	Miss. State, Jackson	14	9
	TOTAL POINTS:	251	298

COACH: Steve Sloan.
CAPTAINS: Eddy Householder, LB; John Peel, DE; Leon Perry, FB.

†Night Game.   ‡TV Game.

1980 — Won 3, Lost 8

Sept. 6	†Texas A&M, Jackson	20	23
Sept. 13	Memphis State, Oxford	61	7
Sept. 20	Alabama, Jackson	35	59
Sept. 27	Tulane, Oxford	24	26
Oct. 4	Southern Miss., Jackson	22	28
Oct. 11	Georgia, Athens	21	28
Oct. 18	Florida, Oxford (HC)	3	15
Oct. 25	Vanderbilt, Nashville	27	14
Nov. 1	‡LSU, Baton Rouge	16	38
Nov. 15	Tennessee, Memphis	20	9
Nov. 22	Miss. State, Jackson	14	19
	TOTAL POINTS:	263	266

COACH: Steve Sloan.
CAPTAINS: Ken Toler, SE; Chuck Commiskey, OG; Joel Stewart, DB.

†Night Game.   ‡TV Game.

1981 — Won 4, Lost 6, Tied 1

Sept. 5	Tulane, New Orleans	19	18
Sept. 12	†South Carolina, Columbia	20	13
Sept. 19	†Memphis State, Memphis	7	3
Sept. 26	†Arkansas, Jackson	13	27
Oct. 3	Alabama, Tuscaloosa	7	38
Oct. 10	Georgia, Oxford	7	37
Oct. 17	Florida, Gainesville	3	49
Oct. 24	Vanderbilt, Oxford (HC)	23	27
Oct. 31	LSU, Jackson	27	27
Nov. 14	Tennessee, Knoxville	20	28
Nov. 21	Miss. State, Jackson	21	17
	TOTAL POINTS:	167	284

COACH: Steve Sloan.
CAPTAIN: John Fourcade, QB.
CO-CAPTAINS: Quentin McDonald, DT; Malvin Gipson, TB.

†Night Game.

1982 — Won 4, Lost 7

Sept. 4	Memphis State, Oxford	27	10
Sept. 11	†Southern Miss., Oxford	28	19
Sept. 18	Alabama, Jackson	14	42
Sept. 25	†Arkansas, Little Rock	12	14
Oct. 9	Georgia, Athens	10	33
Oct. 16	Texas Christian, Oxford (HC)	27	9
Oct. 23	‡Vanderbilt, Nashville	10	19
Oct. 30	†LSU, Baton Rouge	8	45
Nov. 6	†‡Tulane, Jackson	45	14
Nov. 13	Tennessee, Jackson	17	30
Nov. 20	Miss. State, Jackson	10	27
	TOTAL POINTS:	208	262

COACH: Steve Sloan.
CAPTAINS: Nakita Williams, LB; James Otis, LB; Keith Fourcade, LB; Michael Harmon, SE; Steve Herring, C

†Night Game.   ‡TV Game.

1983 — Won 7, Lost 5

Sept. 3	†Memphis State, Memphis	17	37
Sept. 10	*Tulane, New Orleans	23	27
Sept. 17	Alabama, Tuscaloosa	0	40
Sept. 24	†Arkansas, Jackson	13	10
Oct. 1	Southern Miss., Oxford	7	27
Oct. 8	Georgia, Oxford	11	36
Oct. 15	Texas Christian, Ft. Worth	20	7
Oct. 22	Vanderbilt, Oxford (HC)	21	14
Oct. 29	LSU, Jackson	27	24
Nov. 12	†Tennessee, Knoxville	13	10
Nov. 19	Miss. State, Jackson	24	23
	INDEPENDENCE BOWL, Shreveport		
Dec. 10	†Air Force	3	9
	TOTAL POINTS:	179	234

**Won by forfeit.*
COACH: Billy Brewer.
CAPTAINS: Kelly Powell, QB; Buford McGee, TB; Andre Townsend, DT; Dwayne Nesmith, LB.

†Night Game.   ‡TV Game.

1984 — Won 4, Lost 6, Tied 1

Sept. 8	Memphis State, Oxford	22	6
Sept. 15	†Arkansas, Little Rock	14	14
Sept. 22	Louisiana Tech, Oxford	14	8
Sept. 29	Tulane, Oxford (HC)	19	14
Oct. 6	‡Auburn, Oxford	13	17
Oct. 13	‡Georgia, Athens	12	18
Oct. 20	Southern Miss., Jackson	10	13
Oct. 27	Vanderbilt, Nashville	20	37
Nov. 3	†LSU, Baton Rouge	29	32
Nov. 17	Tennessee, Jackson	17	41
Nov. 24	‡Miss. State, Jackson	24	3
	TOTAL POINTS:	194	203

COACH: Billy Brewer.
CAPTAINS: Timmy Moffett, SE; Jamie Holder, FL; Freddie Joe Nunn, DE; Bob Blakemore, DT.

†Night Game.   ‡TV Game.

1985 — Won 4, Lost 6, Tied 1

Sept. 7	†Memphis State, Memphis	17	17
Sept. 14	†Arkansas, Jackson	19	24
Sept. 21	Arkansas State, Oxford	18	16
Sept. 28	†Tulane, New Orleans	27	10
Oct. 5	†‡Auburn, Auburn	0	41
Oct. 12	†Georgia, Jackson	21	49
Oct. 26	Vanderbilt, Oxford (HC)	35	7
Nov. 2	‡LSU, Jackson	0	14
Nov. 9	‡Notre Dame, South Bend	14	37
Nov. 16	‡Tennessee, Knoxville	14	34
Nov. 23	Miss. State, Jackson	45	27
	TOTAL POINTS:	210	276

COACH: Billy Brewer.
CAPTAINS: Jamie Holder, FL; Nathan Wonsley, TB; Jay Webb, DE; Michael Portis, NG; Tony Rayburn, OL.

†Night Game.   ‡TV Game.

1986 — Won 8, Lost 3, Tied 1

Sept. 6	†Memphis State, Jackson	28	6
Sept. 13	†Arkansas, Little Rock	0	21
Sept. 20	Arkansas State, Oxford	10	10
Sept. 27	‡Tulane, Oxford	35	10
Oct. 4	‡Georgia, Athens	10	14
Oct. 11	Kentucky, Jackson	33	13
Oct. 18	Southwestern LA, Oxford	21	20
Oct. 25	Vanderbilt, Nashville	28	12
Nov. 1	‡LSU, Baton Rouge	21	19
Nov. 15	‡Tennessee, Jackson	10	22
Nov. 22	‡Miss. State, Jackson	24	3
	INDEPENDENCE BOWL, Shreveport		
Dec. 20	†‡Texas Tech	20	17
	TOTAL POINTS:	240	167

COACH: Billy Brewer.
CAPTAINS: Jeff Noblin, FS; Mike Fitzsimmons, DT.

†Night Game.   ‡TV Game.

Record In First Year

Flanker Pat Coleman used his first year (1988) as a Rebel to establish a school record with 557 kickoff return yards, which vaulted him into the Top 10 at 9th on the all-time Ole Miss kickoff return list.

1987 — Won 3, Lost 8

Sept. 5	†Memphis State, Memphis	10	16
Sept. 12	†Arkansas, Jackson	10	31
Sept. 19	Arkansas State, Oxford	47	10
Sept. 26	†Tulane, New Orleans	24	31
Oct. 3	Georgia, Oxford	14	31
Oct. 10	†Kentucky, Lexington	6	35
Oct. 17	Southwestern LA, Oxford	24	14
Oct. 24	Vanderbilt, Oxford (HC)	42	14
Oct. 31	†LSU, Jackson	13	42
Nov. 14	Tennessee, Knoxville	13	55
Nov. 21	Miss. State, Jackson	20	30
	TOTAL POINTS:	223	309

COACH: Billy Brewer.
CAPTAINS: Jeff Herrod, LB; Todd Irvin, OT
†*Night Game.*

1988 — Won 5, Lost 6

Sept. 3	†Memphis State, Jackson	24	6
Sept. 10	†Florida, Jackson	15	27
Sept. 17	†Arkansas, Little Rock	13	21
Oct. 1	Georgia, Athens	12	36
Oct. 8	‡Alabama, Tuscaloosa	22	12
Oct. 15	Arkansas State, Oxford	25	22
Oct. 22	Vanderbilt, Nashville	36	28
Oct. 29	‡LSU, Baton Rouge	20	31
Nov. 5	Tulane, Oxford (HC)	9	14
Nov. 12	Tennessee, Oxford	12	20
Nov. 26	Miss. State, Jackson	33	6
	TOTAL POINTS:	221	223

COACH: Billy Brewer.
CAPTAINS: Bryan Owen, K; Wesley Walls, TE; Stevon Moore, CB.
†*Night Game.* ‡*TV Game.*

1989 — Won 8, Lost 4

Sept. 2	†Memphis State, Memphis	20	13
Sept. 9	‡Florida, Gainesville	24	19
Sept. 16	Arkansas State, Oxford	34	31
Sept. 23	†Arkansas, Jackson	17	24
Oct. 7	Alabama, Jackson	27	62
Oct. 14	‡Georgia, Oxford	17	13
Oct. 21	†Tulane, New Orleans	32	28
Oct. 28	Vanderbilt, Oxford (HC)	24	16
Nov. 4	LSU, Oxford	30	35
Nov. 18	Tennessee, Knoxville	21	33
Nov. 25	Miss. State, Jackson	21	11
	LIBERTY BOWL, Memphis		
Dec. 28	†‡Air Force	42	29
	TOTAL POINTS:	309	314

COACH: Billy Brewer
CAPTAINS: Tony Bennett, OLB; Tim Brown, OL; Pat Coleman, WR; John Darnell, QB.
†*Night Game.* ‡*TV Game.*

1990 — Won 9, Lost 3

Sept. 8	†Memphis State, Oxford	23	21
Sept. 15	Auburn, Jackson	10	24
Sept. 22	‡Arkansas, Little Rock	21	17
Sept. 29	Tulane, Oxford	31	21
Oct. 6	‡Kentucky, Oxford	35	29
Oct. 13	‡Georgia, Athens	28	12
Oct. 20	Arkansas State, Oxford (HC)	42	13
Oct. 27	Vanderbilt, Nashville	14	13
Nov. 3	†LSU, Baton Rouge	19	10
Nov. 17	‡Tennessee, Memphis	13	22
Nov. 24	Miss. State, Jackson	21	9
	GATOR BOWL, Jacksonville		
Jan. 1	‡Michigan	3	35
	TOTAL POINTS:	260	226

COACH: Billy Brewer
CAPTAINS: Shawn Cobb, ILB; Chris Mitchell, SS; Kelvin Pritchett, DT; Dawson Pruett, C.
†*Night Game.* ‡*TV Game.*

1991 — Won 5, Lost 6

Aug. 31	°‡Tulane, New Orleans	22	3
Sept. 7	†Memphis State, Memphis	10	0
Sept. 14	†‡Auburn, Auburn	13	23
Sept. 21	†Ohio University, Oxford	38	14
Sept. 28	†Arkansas, Jackson	24	17
Oct. 5	†‡Kentucky, Lexington	35	14
Oct. 12	‡Georgia, Oxford	17	37
Oct. 26	Vanderbilt, Oxford (HC)	27	30
Nov. 2	LSU, Jackson	22	25
Nov. 16	‡Tennessee, Knoxville	25	36
Nov. 23	‡Miss. State, Starkville	9	24
	TOTAL POINTS:	242	223

COACH: Billy Brewer.
CAPTAINS: Darron Billings, RB; Jeff Carter, FS; Cliff Dew, C; Phillip Kent, OLB.
†*Night Game.* ‡*TV Game.* °*First August Date*

1992 — Won 9, Lost 3

Sept. 5	†Auburn, Oxford	45	21
Sept. 12	†Tulane, Oxford	35	9
Sept. 19	†Vanderbilt, Nashville	9	31
Sept. 26	‡Georgia, Athens	11	37
Oct. 3	†Kentucky, Oxford	24	14
Oct. 17	†Arkansas, Little Rock	17	3
Oct. 24	‡Alabama, Tuscaloosa	10	31
Oct. 31	†LSU, Jackson	32	0
Nov. 7	Memphis State (HC), Oxford	17	12
Nov. 14	Louisiana Tech, Oxford	13	6
Nov. 28	‡Mississippi State, Oxford	17	10
	LIBERTY BOWL, Memphis		
Dec. 31	°†‡Air Force	13	0
	TOTAL POINTS:	243	174

COACH: Billy Brewer.
CAPTAINS: Chad Brown, DT; Everett Lindsay, OT; Cory Philpot, TB; Lynn Ross, LB; Russ Shows, QB.
†*Night Game.* ‡*TV Game.*

James A. Autry is a former executive editor of **Better Homes and Gardens** and president of magazine publishing at the Meredith Corporation. A 1957 graduate of Ole Miss, he was inducted into its Alumni Hall of Fame in 1981. His books include Nights Under a Tin Roof, Life After Mississippi and Love and Profit. He lives in Des Moines, Iowa.

John Grisham is a 1981 graduate of Ole Miss Law School. He is the author of A Time to Kill, The Firm, The Pelican Brief and The Client. His bestselling novels have been translated into 21 languages. He lives in Oxford.

Barry Hannah is currently Ole Miss Writer-In-Residence and teaches literature and writing at the University. His books include Geronimo Rex, Airships, Ray, Captain Maximus, The Tennis Handsome, Never Die and Bats Out of Hell. He is a past winner of the American Academy of Arts Award for Fiction.

Willie Morris served as Ole Miss journalist-in-residence from 1980-90 and directed the Visiting Writers Lectureship Program. A former Rhodes Scholar and editor-in-chief of *Harper's,* he is the author of North Toward Home, Terrains of the Heart, The Courting of Marcus Dupree, Good Old Boy and New York Days. He lives in Jackson, Mississippi.

Charles Overby is a former executive editor of The Clarion-Ledger and vice-president of Gannett, Inc. He presently is president of The Freedom Forum in Arlington, Virginia. He studied journalism at Ole Miss and was inducted into the Ole Miss Hall of Fame in 1992.

David Sansing, Professor of History at Ole Miss, was voted Teacher of the Year in 1990 by the student body. His books include Making Haste Slowly, Mississippi History Through Four Centuries and Natchez: An Illustrated History.

Billy Watkins graduated from Ole Miss in 1975. He has received numerous Associated Press awards and three times was named Mississippi Sportswriter of the Year. He is currently a features writer for The Clarion-Ledger.

Dean Faulkner Wells received B.A. and M.A. degrees in English from the University of Mississippi. She is co-publisher at Yoknapatawpha Press in Oxford. Her books include The Ghosts of Rowan Oak, The Great American Writers' Cookbook (editor) and Mississippi Heroes (editor, with Hunter Cole).

Larry Wells received a Ph.D. degree at Ole Miss in 1975. He is co-publisher at Yoknapatawpha Press. He is the author of two novels, Rommell and the Rebel and Let the Band Play Dixie, and edited the photo albums Ole Miss Football, Legend in Crimson and William Faulkner: The Cofield Collection.

William Winter is a 1943 graduate of Ole Miss, where his extra-curricular activities included sports-writing for The Mississippian. His honors include the Associated Press' "Margaret Dixon Freedom of Information Award" and Ole Miss Outstanding Alumnus (1975). He served as governor of Mississippi from 1980-84 and currently practices law in Jackson.

TEAM OF THE CENTURY—
Selected by vote of the Ole
Miss fans, members of the
Team of the Century were
honored with a Black Tie Gala
July 9, 1993. Members of the
team include, front row, from
left, Coach John Vaught,
Charlie Conerly, Barney
Poole, John "Kayo" Dottley,
Larry Grantham, and Marvin
Terrell. Second row, from left,
Gene Hickerson, Stan
Hindman, Archie Manning,
Floyd Franks, Ben Williams,
Robert Khayat, and Charlie
Flowers. Back row, from left,
Todd Sandoni, Jeff Herrod,
Dawson Pruett, Tony Bennett,
Billy Brewer, Jim Dunaway,
Kelvin Pritchett, and Jim
Miller. Team members not
pictured include: Glenn
Cannon, Kenny Dill, Everett
Lindsay, Chris Mitchell,
Freddie Joe Nunn,
Frank"Bruiser" Kinard, and
Jimmy Patton.

UNIVERSITY OF MISSISSIPPI FOOTBALL TEAM OF THE CENTURY

Offense

POS.	NAME	HT.	WT.	YEARS	HOMETOWN
E	Floyd Franks	6-0	190	1968-70	Biloxi, Miss.
E	Barney Poole	6-3	220	1942; '47-48	Gloster, Miss.
OL	Jim Dunaway	6-4	260	1960-62	Columbia, Miss.
OL	Gene Hickerson	6-2	225	1955-57	Atwood, Tenn.
OL	Stan Hindman	6-3	230	1963-65	Newton, Miss.
OL	Everett Lindsay	6-5	290	1989-92	Raleigh, N. C.
OL	Marvin Terrell	6-0	210	1957-59	Indianola, Miss.
C	Dawson Pruett	6-1	269	1987-90	Mobile, Ala.
QB	Archie Manning	6-3	198	1968-70	Drew, Miss.
RB	Charlie Conerly	6-1	183	1942; '46-47	Clarksdale, Miss.
RB	John "Kayo" Dottley	6-0	198	1947-50	McGehee, Ark.
RB	Charlie Flowers	6-0	198	1957-59	Marianna, Ark.
PK	Robert Khayat	6-2	215	1957-59	Moss Point, Miss.

Defense

POS.	NAME	HT.	WT.	YEARS	HOMETOWN
DL	Bruiser Kinard	6-1	215	1935-37	Jackson, Miss.
DL	Kelvin Pritchett	6-3	266	1988-90	Atlanta, Ga.
DL	Ben Williams	6-3	253	1972-75	Yazoo City, Miss.
LB	Tony Bennett	6-2	235	1986-89	Alligator, Miss.
LB	Kenny Dill	6-4	215	1961-63	West Point, Miss.
LB	Larry Grantham	6-0	195	1957-59	Crystal Springs, Miss.
LB	Jeff Herrod	6-0	235	1984-87	Birmingham, Ala.
LB	Freddie Joe Nunn	6-5	227	1981-84	Nanih Waiya, Miss.
DB	Billy Brewer	6-0	190	1957-59	Columbus, Miss.
DB	Glenn Cannon	6-2	182	1967-69	Gulfport, Miss.
DB	Chris Mitchell	6-0	195	1987-90	Town Creek, Ala.
DB	Jimmy Patton	5-11	170	1952-54	Greenville, Miss.
DB	Todd Sandroni	6-1	200	1987-90	Shaw, Miss.
P	Jim Miller	5-11	182	1976-79	Ripley, Miss.

Coach

John Vaught, Head Coach, 1947-70; '73